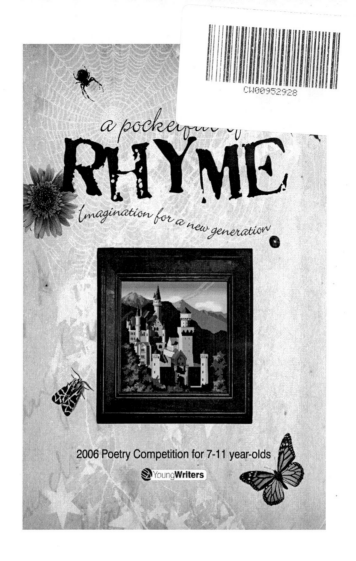

a pocketful of

RHYME

Imagination for a new generation

2006 Poetry Competition for 7-11 year-olds

YoungWriters

Verses From Staffordshire

Edited by Donna Samworth

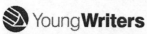 Young**Writers**

First published in Great Britain in 2007 by:
Young Writers
Remus House
Coltsfoot Drive
Peterborough
PE2 9JX
Telephone: 01733 890066
Website: www.youngwriters.co.uk

SB ISBN 1 84602 734 9

Foreword

Young Writers was established in 1991 and has been passionately devoted to the promotion of reading and writing in children and young adults ever since. The quest continues today. Young Writers remains as committed to the nurturing of poetic and literary talent as ever.

This year's Young Writers competition has proven as vibrant and dynamic as ever and we are delighted to present a showcase of the best poetry from across the UK and in some cases overseas. Each poem has been selected from a wealth of *A Pocketful Of Rhyme* entries before ultimately being published in this, our fourteenth primary school poetry series.

Once again, we have been supremely impressed by the overall quality of the entries we have received. The imagination, energy and creativity which has gone into each young writer's entry made choosing the poems a challenging and often difficult but ultimately hugely rewarding task - the general high standard of the work submitted ensured this opportunity to bring their poetry to a larger appreciative audience.

We sincerely hope you are pleased with this final collection and that you will enjoy *A Pocketful Of Rhyme Verses From Staffordshire* for many years to come.

Contents

Carmountside Primary School

Amber Clowes (8)	1
Keenan Mills (8)	1
Shyla Clowes (8)	2
Courtney Louise Machin (8)	2
Emillie Corden (9)	3
Joshua Bradbury (8)	3
Elishia Gaskell (8)	4
Hayleigh Rathbone (9)	4
Jade Whetnall (9)	5
Hector Galbraith (8)	5
Kyle Marsh (8)	6
Catherine Edwards (8)	6

Colwich CE Primary School

Chris Sharp (9)	7
Georgina Allison (10)	8
Carthy Wells (9)	9
Chloe Bedford (10)	10
Laura Pyatt (9)	11
Mark Betteridge (9)	12
Ellie Duffen (9)	13
Matthew Dalton (10)	14
Ben Kenyon (9)	15
Danielle Hatton (10)	16
Jack Sherratt (10)	17
Tom Larkin (9)	18
Kerry Vernon (9)	19
Caiman Toon (9)	20

Five Ways Primary School

Jack Farish (9)	20
Jack Thomas (9)	21
James McDonald (9)	21
Luke Radjenovic (9)	22
Adam Newton (9)	22
Sam Jones (9)	23
Luke Ponder (10)	23
Connor Flavell (9)	24

Ellie-Louise Green (10)   24
Chloe Higginson (9)   25
Eden Smith (9)   25
George Statham (9)   26
Hayley Stokes (9)   26
Molly Dando (9)   27
Alicia Baker (9)   27
Olivia Dawes (9)   28
Lucy Brookes (9)   28
Molly Stapleton (10)   29
Jake Bowdler (9)   30
Samantha Groves (9)   31
Oliver Jukes (9)   32
Ashley Baker (9)   32
Bethany Groves (9)   33
Joe Hunter (9)   33
Matthew Bond (9)   34
Abbie Broadbent (9)   34
Shannon Perkins (9)   35
Olivia Kane (9)   35
James Brown (10)   36
Millie Bell (9)   36
Danielle Jackson (9)   37
Louis McEvoy (9)   37
Emily O'Sullivan (9)   38
Alex Jones (9)   38
Oliver Clark (9)   39
Lauren Parker (9)   39
Scarlett Baker (9)   40
Peter Davis (9)   40
Luke Yeomans-Smith (9)   41
Emily Lycett (10)   41
Emily Bradburn (9)   42
Jack Garner (9)   42
Eleanor Dewsbury (10)   43
Ryan Higginson (11)   43
Thomas Birch (9)   44
Jack Dace (9)   45
Matthew Joyce (9)   45
Andy Spurr (9)   46
Kieran Meredith (9)   46
Shannon David (10)   47

Edward Evans (9)	47
Ben Watson (10)	48
Bradley Woodhouse (9)	48
Sam Nutting (9)	49
Joe Emery (9)	49
Adam Tolladay (9)	50
Lauren Tonks (9)	50
Sophie Woodall (10)	51
Gabrielle Purshouse (9)	51
Charlotte Brindley (9)	52
Elliot Woolley (10)	52
Amy Grace Baker (9)	53
Ashley Sumner (10)	53
Rebecca Purchase (10)	54
Chantelle Burton (10)	54
Ryan Phillips (9)	55
Ryan Arnold (10)	55
James Statham (9)	56
Matthew Jones (9)	56
Jonathan Whitbread (10)	57
James Evans (9)	57
Rachael Collins (10)	58
Kelly Pugh (9)	58
Calum Gallier (10)	59
Jack Terry (9)	59
Lucy Gladston (11)	60
Tom Showell (9)	60
Harry Clinton (10)	61
Matt Olorenshaw (10)	61
Owen Jenkinson (9)	62
Adam Scargill (9)	62
Matthew Round (10)	63
Danielle Samson (9)	63
Megan Atkinson (9)	64
Hannah Lote (10)	64

Hayes Meadow Primary School

Michael McGann (10)	65
Courtney Stockle	65
Mia Parry	65
Megan McMeel	66

Callum McComisky (9)	66
Josef Bogunovic (10)	66
Mason Joyce (11)	67
Chloe Andrea	67
Joshua Duffy	67
Emily Fisher	68
Megan Young (9)	68
Joshua Cornes (9)	68
Ben Yates	69
Kerry Baily (10)	69

Lichfield Cathedral School

Daniel Kinsella (8)	70
Annabel Forrest-King (8)	70
Jessica Shaw (8)	70
Finley Saunders (8)	71
Beth Jacob (8)	72
Natasha Rowland-Lovett (9)	72
Fern Bradley (8)	72
Chloe Newton (8)	73
Eleanor Proudlove (9)	73
Molly Beharrell (9)	74
Harry Whiting (9)	74
Nicholas Kearns (8)	75
Andrew Murphy (7)	75
Isabella James (8)	75
Hannah Lawson (7)	76
Minnie Butlin (7)	76
Archie Hulse (7)	76
Francesca York (7)	77
Maxim Hibbs (8)	77
Simon Ashwood (7)	77
Molly Dell (9)	78
Robert McIntosh (8)	78
Victoria Gough (8)	79
James Lloyd (9)	79
Madeleine Sanders (8)	80
William Harvey (8)	80
Henry Southan (8)	81
Olivia Thackray (8)	81
Elliott Manley (7)	81

Lottie Pike (8)	82
Nicole Higgins (8)	82
Alex Wakefield (8)	83
Richard Chapman (7)	83
Siobhan Carlin (8)	84
Oliver Chatham (8)	84
Julian Patient (7)	85
Sam Dewsbery (7)	85
James Wyatt (7)	86
Tommie Collingwood (7)	86
Freddie Beharrell (7)	86
Lauren James (7)	87
William Mucklow (7)	87
Annika Rabone (7)	87
Dominic Sterland (7)	88
Oona McBride (8)	88
Lauren Ward (7)	89
Isobel Butler (7)	89
Otto Williams (8)	90
Alice-Ruth Davies (7)	90
Darcy Banks & Amelia Sanders (7)	91
Dan Wakefield & William Collins (8)	91
Molly Hudson & Matthew Inglis (7)	92

St Luke's CE Primary School, Cannock

Joe Murphy (10)	92
Jacob Massey (11)	93
Chloe Smith (10)	94
Will Gonsalves (10)	95
Alex Lloyd (10)	96
Christie Ghent (10)	97
Sam Whitehouse (10)	98
Connor Taylor (10)	99
Katie Barnes (10)	100
William Hawkins (11)	101
Rachel Beaman (10)	102
Ellen Whordley (10)	103
Amy McKenzie (10)	104
Jack Plester (11)	104
David Cockram (10)	105
Shaun Gilbert (10)	105

Emma Watkins (10)   106
Alice Standley (10)   107
Bethany Evans (10)   108
Kira George (10)   109
William Bakewell (11)   110
Chanelle Tranter (11)   111
Connor Bates (10)   112
Megan Shirley (10)   113
Amber Parkes (10)   114
Jessica Hodgkiss (10)   115
Kieran Evans (11)   116
Bradley Davies (10)   116
Katie O'Mahoney (10)   117
Philip Bell (10)   117
Abi Cartwright (10)   118
Daniel Hyde (10)   119
Rowen Wort (10)   120
Christopher Keeley (10)   121
Dionne Drysdale (10)   122
Zach Harrison (10)   123
Nick Allen (10)   124
Elliott Thurstance (10)   125
Adam Cardno (10)   126
Jade McLaughlin (10)   127
Ryan McCulloch (10)   128
Sam Figurski (10)   129
Megan Thompson (10)   130
Jack Wright (11)   131
Richard Jones (11)   132
Siobhan Bradbury (10)   133
Samuel Diesbergen (10)   134

St Peters Primary School, Yoxall

Ross Perry (7)   134
Katie Burbridge (7)   135
Emily Cleary (8)   135
Ellen Rutherford (8)   136
James Bell (7)   136
Harvey Marples (7)   137
Lydia Hart (8)   137
Robert Carr (8)   138

Hanna Fletcher (7)   138
Lauren Wood (8)   139
Francesca Browne (8)   139

The Mosley Primary School
Eleana O'Hare (9)   140
Callum Gibson (9)   140
Natasha Ebbutt (9)   141
Caitlin Wright (9)   141
Matthew Holmes (10)   142
Lewis Brittain (9)   143
Kyla Hyslop (10)   144
Annabelle Eaton (10)   145
Adam Parsons (9)   146
Rachel Frame (11)   147
Eleanor Bradley (9)   148
Ben Barrett (10)   148

The Poems

Outside

It's dark outside
The wind is howling like a wolf
I'm so terrified my hair spikes up

The branches on the trees are swaying
They look like a scary monster coming to get me!

Argh! This is freaking me out!
Twigs creaking under my shoes
I hear strange noises from a distance

Can't take anymore
I slam the door, shut my eyes
And drift off
Into a deep, deep outside sleep.

Amber Clowes (8)
Carmountside Primary School

Outside

Cold and icy trampoline
Nobody to play with
A stripy orange tiger creeping past the shed
Me shivering with fright
The trees rattling, fighting against the wind
The petrol taste in my mouth as cars zoom
Dogs snapping at their shadows
Breeze-filled petrol going up my nostrils
Insects talking in the bushes
Leaves crunching when people walk
Closing the door leaving the outside, outside.

Keenan Mills (8)
Carmountside Primary School

Outside

Great statues staring straight at me,
Frozen!
Is there anyone to help us?
A stripy cat stamps on a snail.
I feel so angry and sad.
Then it pounces on the fence and prowls away.
Why did she do that?
A cold breeze catches my nostrils.
The smell of fumes.
Standing on crunchy leaves.
Sounds of the night.
I shut my door, close my eyes.
Wave the night goodbye
As I drift away.

Shyla Clowes (8)
Carmountside Primary School

Outside

Wet and icy swings
Is anybody going to swing on them?
Breezy sour taste in my mouth
Stripy tiger cats on my grass creeping up to my trampoline
A cold breezy night is petrol through my nostrils
Thunder in the dark
Streak of lightning comes at me
Leaves scratching, people talking
Insects screeching
The sound of the night outside.

Courtney Louise Machin (8)
Carmountside Primary School

Outside

The day begins
The branches creaking
Helicopters circling
Tasting the breeze
Birds whistling merrily
Beautiful butterflies flying all around

Dark night begins
Slow snails slithering through my garden
Bats swooping and soaring
Crickets croaking
Will I ever get to sleep?
Trees hustling, making spooky shapes in my head
'Muuuummm!'
Night has come!

Emillie Corden (9)
Carmountside Primary School

Outside

The rain is wet
The rain is cold
It makes big puddles
By the side of the road
I can put on my wellies
And splash my way home
I can have fun
And get soaked to the bone
The water drips off the end of my nose
I can feel the cold to the end of my toes.

Joshua Bradbury (8)
Carmountside Primary School

Outside

The night sky caught my eye
The sky sparkles with delight
I'm scared, nowhere to go
Smells of town air coming by

The taste of sweets in my mouth
Smelling fresh like my best friends
Stars so bright filling the frame
Autumn leaves floating down
Cold sour taste in my mouth

Sounds from outside coming in my bedroom
The howling of the wind
My eyes are closed
Daytime thoughts have gone
Night-time sleep has come.

Elishia Gaskell (8)
Carmountside Primary School

Outside

The benches creaking
Is anybody going to sit on me?
Worriedness in my mouth
A dog howling next door
The chain moving as the big dog prowls
Trees blowing very fast indeed
Burning fire, burning, smelling of gas
The dark night appearing in my bedroom
Spooky monster-shapes making a circle around my head
Snails crunching as people tread on them
People shouting loud while insects dance
The thoughts of outside.

Hayleigh Rathbone (9)
Carmountside Primary School

Outside

Wet clothes hanging there on a washing line
Stripy cat creeping through the gardens
Who knows where he or she is going
A fly trying to get in

A flag drooping against the pole
I can see flowers sitting sadly in the ground
A bird bath brimming full with water
Gnomes surrounding the bird bath

Shimmering rooftops with rain
Shapes, different sizes and coloured sheds
Trees far and near
Squish goes the slug as I tread on it
Light time, night-time, bed time.

Jade Whetnall (9)
Carmountside Primary School

Outside

Frogs croaking, grass long
My swing creaking in the cold breeze
Rainy slides and icy grass
Cars beeping in queues, rustling bonfires crackling
Monster shadows through my window
Insects chanting, leaves crunching
Water splashing in the pond
Birds singing somewhere in the trees
Clocks ticking, music frightening
Feet pattering against the ground
Cats prowling, dogs howling
The smell of the outside
Outside at night.

Hector Galbraith (8)
Carmountside Primary School

Outside

Chestnut trees feeling lonely and damp
The freezing taste of ice in my slimy mouth
Dogs growling at the gate
Prowling straight towards me!
Frightening smell of angry dogs swarming around my head
Night brings strange wheezing sounds and spooky shadows
Thunder, lightning striking things
Ripped bark
Trees missing leaves, everywhere leaves crunching
Strange wheezing sounds
Sounds of the outside.

Kyle Marsh (8)
Carmountside Primary School

Outside

Crunching leaves, wheezing people
Dogs howling at the moon
Will anyone make them stop?

Taste of petrol in my mouth
'Ouch!' said the step when I sat on it
Looking at the starry sky

Aeroplane zooming high
Around, all shapes, spooky!
Goodnight world
Feelings of the outside!

Catherine Edwards (8)
Carmountside Primary School

The Magic Box

(Based on 'Magic Box' by Kit Wright)

I will put in the box . . .
A beautiful high speed sports car,
A great white shark leaping out of the
Pacific Ocean
A diamond from the deepest mine in Africa.

I will put in the box . . .
A star as giant as a lorry,
A ray of golden sunlight,
A multicoloured scorpion from the biggest desert in Egypt.

I will put in the box . . .
The night sky on a summer night,
A spotted cheetah's head on a lion's back,
A bar of the creamiest chocolate from Thornton's in sixty year's time.

I will put in the box . . .
A giant, meat-eating dinosaur,
A dragonfly with the shiniest eyes,
And my first ever teddy.

My box is fashioned from
Dragon scales and knight's armour,
It has corners made of red diamonds
And the hinges are made of emerald dragon wings.

I shall ride in my box
On the fastest skateboard
Speed down a ramp,
Leap over a river
And land safely on the other side.

Chris Sharp (9)
Colwich CE Primary School

The Magic Box

(Based on 'Magic Box' by Kit Wright)

I will put in the box . . .
A white witch galloping through swaying corn,
The strong breeze of a whistling wind,
Lush flowers from a sweet-smelling meadow.

I will put in the box . . .
The bluest water from the best river,
The rain from the darkest rooftop,
The cold air from a mild sky

I will put in the box . . .
The runniest chocolate in the world,
The most wonderful smell of scented roses
A clap of thunder from a winter's day

My box is fashioned from gold and silver,
Flashes of lightning cover the lid,
Its hinges are made from stars

I shall dance in my box
On the highest stage with the brightest lights,
With the big brown velvet curtain
To the claps and cheers of the crowd.

Georgina Allison (10)
Colwich CE Primary School

The Magic Box

(Based on 'Magic Box' by Kit Wright)

I will put in the box . . .
The first drop of blood from a fallen tooth,
A bar of the most fantastic chocolate ever made,
The most colourful, shiny bubbles ever blown.

I will put in the box . . .
A pony eating grass in a meadow,
The bluest eyes ever,
A lion cub asleep with its mother.

I will put in the box . . .
The beautiful feeling of drinking fresh, blue water,
A star that glistens at night,
The smell of a cold winter's day.

My box is fashioned from fast flowing water,
Icicles dropping from the ceiling,
Its hinges are mermaids twisting and turning in water.

In my box I shall fly
And soar through the air,
Then I shall have a doze on a cotton cloud.

Carthy Wells (9)
Colwich CE Primary School

The Magic Box

(Based on 'Magic Box' by Kit Wright)

I will put in the box . . .
A shimmering black horse,
A glittering diamond ring,
The silkiest scale of a fish.

I will put in the box . . .
A powerful slithering snake,
A long, twisted skipping rope,
The fluffiest red bear.

I will put in the box . . .
A golden palace with a prince and princess,
A sip of the bluest pond
And a sizzling blood-red candle.

I will put in the box . . .
A baby's first smile,
A flame from the first ever dragon,
My first ever shoe.

My box is fashioned from a glittering picture of a castle,
With the silkiest velvet on the lid,
Its hinges are four golden wishes.

I shall dance in my box
Through sunrise and sunset
And the people will applaud until the final curtain call.

Chloe Bedford (10)
Colwich CE Primary School

The Magic Box

(Based on 'Magic Box' by Kit Wright)

I will put in the box . . .
A blazing fire that raises high into the dark night sky,
A sharp shining tooth of a shark,
Golden eggs from the finest hens.

I will put in the box . . .
A shiny key that will lead you to the temple of treasures,
The laugh of a baby,
A petal from the first ever flower.

I will put in the box . . .
A piece of shining armour from the strongest knight,
A ray of the hottest sun,
A pearl from the most colourful oyster.

I will put in the box . . .
A kiss from the most luscious lips,
A touch of pink fairy dust,
A bone from a scary dragon.

My box is fashioned from
Clear blue water,
On all the sides fairies dance inside their marble cases,
Its hinges are made from cats' ears.

I shall float in my box as high
As the sky
And fall into the highest room of the tallest tower.

Laura Pyatt (9)
Colwich CE Primary School

The Magic Box

(Based on 'Magic Box' by Kit Wright)

I will put in the box . . .
The sweet smell of a teddy bear's picnic,
A cow jumping over the creamiest white moon,
And the shiny stars that lead you home.

I will put in the box . . .
The great taste of my first ever dark creamy chocolate bar,
The beautiful sound of a steam train in the moonlight,
And the wonderful smell of fresh bread

I will put in the box . . .
The freezing feeling from the first time it snowed,
And the scarecrow that scares the birds away.

My box is fashioned from
The shiniest ruby and silver jewellery,
The lid is covered with fire and the bottom is covered with water,
Its hinges are made from cows' tails.

I shall run in my box on the longest track
With the fastest runners from the Olympics,
As I cross the finish line the crowd will cheer
And all eyes will be on me.

Mark Betteridge (9)
Colwich CE Primary School

The Magic Box

(Based on 'Magic Box' by Kit Wright)

I will put in the box . . .
The touch of cool, cold water touching my crinkled lips,
The golden, red sun glowing warmly on my smooth skin,
The sight of a cat racing through the air.

I will put in the box . . .
The scent of wild red roses that smell of perfume,
The feeling of a smooth soft bear,
The sight of an animal climbing up a tree.

I will put in the box . . .
The smell of the creamiest, most delicious chocolate,
The fruitiest flavoured milkshake,
The feel of the softest, furriest coat.

My box is fashioned from moving fairy-tale pictures,
In the corners there are items from four fairy tales,
Its hinges are made out of princess' silky dresses.

I shall travel in my box
Through the hottest deserts where the sun always shines,
I will end on a deserted island,
Surrounded by the clearest, coolest water.

Ellie Duffen (9)
Colwich CE Primary School

The Magic Box

(Based on 'Magic Box' by Kit Wright)

I will put in the box . . .
The smell of the first ever Mars bar,
The feel of Mickey Mouse's glove,
The warmth of the sun's hottest rays

I will put in the box . . .
The smell of smoke that came out of the very first rocket,
The comfort of my dad's hugs,
The coldness of Pluto.

I will put in the box . . .
The feel of my first clothes,
The smell of my very first PlayStation game,
The warmth of my first bed

My box is fashioned from gold rubies
And glamorous red sapphire
The lid is made out of marbles with the
Solar system in them
Its hinges are made out of a Hungarian horntail's wings.

I will sing in my box
The song of holiday to great applause,
Get thrown into the crowd and
They will carry me across to my glorious exit.

Matthew Dalton (10)
Colwich CE Primary School

The Magic Box

(Based on 'Magic Box' by Kit Wright)

I will put in the box . . .
The iron fang of a sleek grey wolf,
The trancing glare of a worn out watch,
A sip of the ruby lava from the highest volcano
And the foaming smell of a gorgeous hot chocolate.

I will put in the box . . .
A freezing tip of a sapphire icicle,
The volcanic burn of a fired candle
And a cute feather of a blue tit.

I will put in the box . . .
A smooth scale of a horntail dragon,
The bone-hard club of a troll
And the sharp sword of a goblin.

My box is fashioned from emerald, light and bone,
Its hinges are slot machines
And its lock is made of the fangs of a yeti.

I shall bring my box alive,
Allow the wolves to howl,
The dragons to roam free
And the lava to whirl around the world.

Ben Kenyon (9)
Colwich CE Primary School

The Magic Box

(Based on 'Magic Box' by Kit Wright)

I will put in the box . . .
A dazzling flicker of a blood-red candle,
A blazing ray of sun that's coloured golden, black and green,
A cheetah racing wildly through the great jungle.

I will put in the box . . .
A radiant laser coloured deep blue like the Red Sea,
A beautiful lavender star that shines in the night sky,
A gorgeous view of Lyme Regis.

I will put in the box . . .
The smell of dark chocolate melting in my mouth,
The soft touch of a white rose,
The sound of waves lapping against the cliffs.

I will put in the box . . .
The frozen wind hitting against my face,
The enchanted sun beaming in my eyes,
The tender smell of triple chocolate cake.

My box is fashioned from red sapphires,
Blue emeralds and green rubies that glisten,
The lid has dancing pixies in clear, diamond cases,
Its hinges are made of tiny literacy books that glow in the dark.

I shall live in my box
And invite all my friends to a posh party
And when the party ends, we will take a trip on the Titanic.

Danielle Hatton (10)
Colwich CE Primary School

The Magic Box

(Based on 'Magic Box' by Kit Wright)

I will put in my box . . .
The feel of the first time I touched water,
The smooth taste of my first ever chocolate bar,
The smell of freshly baked bread from the bakery.

I will put in my box . . .
The smell of chlorine in a swimming pool,
The feeling of my first step,
The smell of a full English breakfast.

I will put in my box . . .
The sweet feel of a baby's hand,
The fantastic smell of walking into McDonald's,
The soft feeling of my first ever teddy bear.

I will put in my box . . .
A light night sky and a dark sun,
The finest scale from a dinosaur's head,
The smell of my first ever sweets.

My box is fashioned from the Queen's best jewellery,
The corners are made from everlasting wishes,
Its hinges are made from fire-breathing dragon's wings.

I shall cycle in my box upon the fastest track,
The wind rushing through my hair,
Pulling my brakes as I cross the finish line.

Jack Sherratt (10)
Colwich CE Primary School

The Magic Box

(Based on 'Magic Box' by Kit Wright)

I will put in the box . . .
The cry of a newborn baby,
A dog playing with a cat,
And a cowboy driving a motorbike.

I will put in the box . . .
A ray of the brightest sun,
Dust from the hottest desert.

I will put in the box . . .
A flag from the atlas
Fluff from the softest blanket,
And a tooth from the biggest shark.

My box is fashioned from blue fire and red water,
And has love in the corners,
Its hinges are made from dragon teeth.

I shall fly in my box
Like a bird in the bluest sky,
Then land in a lovely green field,
On a lovely summer's morning.

Tom Larkin (9)
Colwich CE Primary School

The Magic Box

(Based on 'Magic Box' by Kit Wright)

I will put in the box . . .
The name 'Diamond Sagle'
A lock of hair from the first horse I rode,
My old rabbit Blackie.

I will put in the box . . .
The bubbles of excitement frothing in my mouth,
A golden ray of sunshine,
The first gap between my teeth.

I will put in the box . . .
The first gherkin I tasted at McDonald's
The feel of dough when I bake a cake,
The taste of gravy on Christmas Day.

My box is fashioned from a ball of fire with love enclosed by a
human heart
wishes in all five corners,
the hinges are wolves' fangs.

I will ride in my box
On the rockiest roller coaster
Then come off with my face as red as a rose bush.

Kerry Vernon (9)
Colwich CE Primary School

The Magic Box

(Based on 'Magic Box' by Kit Wright)

I will put in the box . . .
The roasting golden sun on a summer's day,
The taste of my first ever birthday cake,
The colours of a sparkling firework in the dark night sky.

I will put in the box . . .
The comfort of a nice, cosy bed,
Indian spices
And the loveliest, creamiest chocolate.

My box is fashioned from chrome-plated silver with lots of jewels,
There are surprises in the corners,
Its hinges are dragon's tails.

I shall travel in my box
Across the biggest and hottest deserts
And have a relaxing time.

Caiman Toon (9)
Colwich CE Primary School

Favourite Seasons

Winter
As the crisp white snow fell,
It lay still like a white blanket
And children threw glistening
Snowballs through mid-air
And the cold travelled around the town
Nights grew darker
Trees were bare.

Spring
After winter daffodils grow on
The fields and new life begins
Lambs in the fields and a spring in their step
The air is crisp but the sun shines
The days grow longer, nights grow shorter.

Jack Farish (9)
Five Ways Primary School

Super Seasons

Summer, summer coming fast
Six weeks holiday soon goes past
Away in Spain, hot, hot sun
Sand and sea, lots of fun!

Mornings lighter, nights so dark,
Autumn's coming hear the larks
Leaves are falling much too soon,
What comes next, winter moon.

Snow is falling, whiter than white
Icy roads give you a fright
Christmas comes and new year goes
Into spring and the flowers grow.

Budding daffs and crocus bulbs,
Warmer days and cheeks that glow.
Summer's coming, here we go
Start again our seasons flow.

Jack Thomas (9)
Five Ways Primary School

Autumn

Leaves are turning colours as they sit
On the tree waiting to fall down

Conker shells are cracking
Kids coming inside as the days get darker

Brown leaves falling
Swiftly through the cold damp air

Kids start to go to school wearing coats
As the days get colder

Window screens frosting as autumn is
Coming to an end and winter is starting.

James McDonald (9)
Five Ways Primary School

Seasons Poem

Spring is new leaves growing
Spring is new lambs
Spring is the daffodil season
Spring is Easter time.

Summer is hot
Summer is the summer holidays
Summer is bright nights
Summer is picnics.

Autumn is leaves falling off trees
Autumn is Bonfire Night
Autumn is Hallowe'en
Autumn is all the animals storing their food.

Winter is Christmas
Winter is very cold
Winter is snow
Winter is dark.

Luke Radjenovic (9)
Five Ways Primary School

Seasons Poem

Spring is new leaves growing
Spring is new lambs
Spring is the daffodil season
Spring is Easter time.

Summer is holiday season
Summer is long nights
Summer is sunny season.

Autumn is falling leaves
Autumn is conker season.

Winter is snow season
Winter is Christmas Day.

Adam Newton (9)
Five Ways Primary School

Seasons

Spring is new leaves growing
Spring is new lambs
Spring is the daffodil season
Spring is Easter time.

Summer is about sun
Summer is about hot days
Summer is lots of flowers
Summer is bees making honey

Autumn is lots of rain
Autumn is trees losing leaves
Autumn is dark nights
Autumn is lots of daddy-long-legs

Winter is snow
Winter is lots of rain
Winter is cold days
Winter is my favourite season.

Sam Jones (9)
Five Ways Primary School

Sandy The Snowman

Sandy the snowman,
Fat and small
Watches the children playing snowball.

Sandy the snowman
He's there all day,
But how he would like to run and play.

Sandy the snowman,
Will melt and go,
And all he leaves is a lump of snow.

Sandy the snowman,
Everyone's friend
And he will be there right till the end.

Luke Ponder (10)
Five Ways Primary School

Seasons Poem

Spring is new leaves growing
Spring is new lambs
Spring is daffodil season
Spring is Easter time.

Summer is a nice day
Summer is holidays
Summer is flowers blooming
Summer is eating ice lollies.

Autumn is leaves dropping
Autumn is finding conkers
Autumn is cold weather coming
Autumn is the trees bare.

Winter is Christmas time
Winter is snow on the ground
Winter is time to wear coats and hats
Winter is making snowmen.

Connor Flavell (9)
Five Ways Primary School

Sunny Spring

Spring is a welcoming time of year
When baby animals and flowers appear
The blossom opens on the trees
While birds make a nest of twigs and leaves
Bulbs start sprouting out of the soil
And curly grass starts to coil
Farmers start to sow their seeds
For the crops to grow and hover in the gentle breeze
With birds singing all day long
That shows that spring is an endless song.

Ellie-Louise Green (10)
Five Ways Primary School

Seasons Poem

Spring is new leaves
Spring is new daffodils
Spring is new lambs
Spring is Easter.

Summer is new sunshine
Summer is new buds
Summer is nice and hot
Summer is new holidays
Summer is new butterflies.

Autumn is new bare trees
Autumn is new rainy showers
Autumn is new Hallowe'en
Autumn is new leaves
Autumn is new conkers.

Winter is new icicles
Winter is new snow
Winter is new pantomime
Winter is new cosy nights
Winter is new Christmas.

Chloe Higginson (9)
Five Ways Primary School

Seasons

Weather is a funny thing
It's often rainy in the spring
Summer, hot and very sunny
Flowers bloom and bees make honey,
In Autumn the leaves are falling down
Kids jump in piles on the ground
Winter has a lot of snow
So, hop on a sleigh
Come on, let's go!

Eden Smith (9)
Five Ways Primary School

Seasons Poem

Spring is new leaves growing
Spring is new lambs
Spring is the daffodil season
Spring is Easter time.

Summer is sunny and hot,
I like to ride my bike a lot
I go on holiday every year
Go on the sand and see if it's clear

Autumn is leaves falling down
From the trees upon the ground.
Some little animals hibernate.
Lots of birds will migrate.

Winter is full of joy
Because at Christmas we get lots of toys
It snow should fall upon the ground
It looks like a cloud.

George Statham (9)
Five Ways Primary School

Autumn's Begun

Golden leaves are falling
Winter days are calling
Birds are migrating
Hedgehogs are hibernating
The pumpkin's eyes are twinkling
Children are trick or treating
The bonfire is alight
The rockets screech into the sky
But although it's cold outside when I see my friends
I feel warm inside.

Hayley Stokes (9)
Five Ways Primary School

Season Poems

Spring is new leaves growing
Spring is new lambs
Spring is the daffodil season
Spring is Easter time.

Summer is the sunny season
Summer is shorts time
Summer is barbeque
Summer is holiday time

Autumn is the fall of leaves
Autumn is Hallowe'en and bonfire
Autumn is conker season
Autumn is the end of summer.

Winter is the cold season.
Winter is warm clothes
Winter is making snowmen
Winter is Christmas time.

Molly Dando (9)
Five Ways Primary School

Summer Times

My favourite time of the year is near,
Spring has gone and summer is here.

Time to visit the beach again,
Sun, sea and sand are coming my way.

The barbecue is ready, sausages are sizzling,
Seagulls above are loud and whistling.

The day draws to a close, sand in our toes,
What magnificent days were those.

Alicia Baker (9)
Five Ways Primary School

Autumn

In autumn the leaves on the trees are red, yellow and brown
Summer sunshine has gone, but let's not frown
As autumn too has some delight, Hallowe'en and Bonfire Night
But the best bit of autumn is for me
Hidden high in a horse chestnut tree.
Growing all spiky, green and plump waiting to fall
To the ground with a bump . . .
Conkers!
When they are ripe they split and swell
You pull them from their spiky shell
Then take them home and put them on a string
As tomorrow a contest is happening
We'll bash each other's conkers with all our might
Like the two conkers are having a fight
The winner will be laughing as their conker
Is still left on the string.

Olivia Dawes (9)
Five Ways Primary School

Winter!

I looked out of my window,
A new season had just begun.
Snowflakes flew past my eyes,
I ran outside, snowmen surrounded me,
I felt like I was being guarded by huge chunks of snow.
I ducked as a snowball came zooming towards me.
It came from a snowball fight from up the road.
They were having so much fun.
I felt like joining in, but I didn't know them.
My friends and I lay down on the snowy ground.
We made snow angels.

Later, we sat drinking hot chocolate with cookies,
Wishing that the snow would never melt away . . .

Lucy Brookes (9)
Five Ways Primary School

Winter Tree

Bowing down to the howling winds of winter,
My twisted branches groaning painfully
My gnarled bark all knotted and ancient,
Yearning to feel the sunlight on my stiff frozen body
Given up all hope of spring.

Once I was so beautiful - spring feels so long ago
When my blossom spread along my delicate branches,
Like an elegant shawl of silk draped across my boughs.
People stopped to admire me, I stood proud and tall
I danced in the gentle spring breeze.

Summer came; I wore a magnificent coat of green
Children noisily swung from my strong branches
Families picnicked in the welcome shade of my foliage
As the birds sang in beautiful harmony
I had a purpose.

Golden, purple, red and orange, were my fragile clothes
They shrivelled away and left me bare
Blown away by the sharp winds of autumn
My seeds dropping to the ground, twirling, tumbling silently
The future generation - my children.

Now here I stand, lonely, old, useless
The cruel winter winds chilling me to the core
My once beautiful boughs hanging heavily with snow
As the clouds race across the moon I feel myself drifting off to sleep
I am dying.

Molly Stapleton (10)
Five Ways Primary School

Seasons

Seasons come again and again,
They never stop, it's all the same
Spring, summer, autumn also
Then finally winter that brings the snow.

Spring
I absolutely love spring
Spring is the time when the birds sing
The flowers open, the trees grow
The ice melts and the rivers flow.

Summer
Summer is the sunshine season
We all break up from school
We go on holiday and have some fun
I jump in the pool.

Autumn
Autumn's when the wind starts to blow
The leaves turn gold and red
The hedgehog goes to hibernate
As he curls up in his bed.

Winter
The winter's when the snow falls
We have snow fights with snowballs
Snowmen come as we make them well
From the frozen snow that has fell.

Jake Bowdler (9)
Five Ways Primary School

Seasons

S un is getting stronger
P lants are starting to flower and
R ising from the ground
I t is getting warmer
N ew animals being born
G amboling lambs

S un is at its highest
U nderneath the huge oak tree for shade
M ulticoloured gardens
M ost schools are having a holiday
E ndless playing in the sun
R elaxing in the warm summer heat.

A nimals hibernating
U mbrellas at the ready
T rees are turning gold and red
U mbrellas at the ready
M emories of the long summer we had
N ow the nights are getting darker.

W ater is freezing
I cicles hang sharp and steer
N ow Santa is watching over us
T rees decorated for Christmas
E nd of the year
R eindeer flying high up in the sky.

Samantha Groves (9)
Five Ways Primary School

Winter

Snow starts appearing
Snowmen are made,
Dark nights are coming
Days are getting shorter
Gloomy weather comes with hail and snow.

Trees are put up,
Decorated with shiny tinsel and colourful baubles,
Tuneful carols are sung,
We celebrate the day
Christ was born.

Hip, hip hooray!
New Year again,
Fireworks and loud explosions light up the night sky
Big Ben chimes at midnight,
An old year out, a new year in.

Not as much joy
Coming is spring
Decorations are put down
Snow turns to mushy slush
Winter is over again.

Oliver Jukes (9)
Five Ways Primary School

Autumn Winds

As I was walking down the street
Something fell beside my feet
Leaves carelessly dancing
In the crisp autumn air
Brown, yellow, red and green
And that is all I saw

Autumn is here once again
Leaves are falling one by one
Children are playing and the sun has begun.

Ashley Baker (9)
Five Ways Primary School

Seasons

Scorching hot sun
Paddling pools out
Swimming costumes on
Summer

Leaves on trees
Red, brown and orange
Leaves on the floor
Autumn

Snow on the floor
Snowmen about,
Trees gleaming white
Winter.

Lambs being born
Flowers spring
Leaves come back on trees
Spring.

Bethany Groves (9)
Five Ways Primary School

Winter

Winter is snow falling
Softly to the ground
Winter is bare trees
Covered in snow
Winter is ducks
Sliding on frozen ponds
Winter is ice-cold air
Blowing sharply across your face
Winter is excited kids
Waiting for Christmas.

Joe Hunter (9)
Five Ways Primary School

My Summer Holidays

Summertime here we come
The sun blazing down
Swirling round my brain, beach and sandcastles
America right in my eyes
Rockets away at the Kennedy Space Centre
A pool all to ourselves
Fun all around me
The six weeks off were here
Loud noises from the rides.

Nan going round the house
My birthday and my face lit up
Games with my nan, 'Sorry' 'Scrabble'
Restaurants every twice a week
Fun and games at 'Chase It' for two weeks
But before you know it, it was back to school.

Matthew Bond (9)
Five Ways Primary School

Winter Wonderland

Soft snowdrops floating from the sky
Plump, round snowmen
Rooftops covered in sparkling snow
Snowball fights
Sharp icicles pointing down,
Sledging down a steep hill
The attack of Jack Frost
Wrapped up from head to toe
Prickly holly on front doors
Decorating Christmas trees
The jolly man in the famous red suit
The joy of Christmas morning
Robin red breast
Sipping creamy hot chocolate and
Best of all a warm, crackling fire!

Abbie Broadbent (9)
Five Ways Primary School

Seasons

Sunny Summer
Summer is a time for splashing in the pool
Summer is not a time for school
Every day we have such fun
Playing in the burning hot summer sun

Autumn
Autumn sees the leaves fall down
Crisp, red and golden-brown
Pumpkin pies and witches' cakes
Look what Hallowe'en makes

Winter
Winter is a time for wrapping up warm
This is the month that Jesus was born
Presents surround the Christmas tree
What's inside? Wait and see.

Spring
Spring is here, wait and see
Newborn lambs jumping free
Daffodils and tulips grow
The farmer has his seeds to sow.

Shannon Perkins (9)
Five Ways Primary School

Seasons

Having Fun In The Blazing Hot Sun

Summer is about having fun
Playing with your friends in the hot summer sun
Playing in the sea in your swimsuit
Beautiful flowers spread all over the ground.

Winter Has Come

Winter is when you walk across the white, soft crunchy snow
People are wearing coats scarves and warm, woolly gloves
Children skate over the slippery ice.

Olivia Kane (9)
Five Ways Primary School

Seasons

S un rises after the cold winter
R ain starts to stop
P lants begin to grow
I cicles are no more
N ow leaves begin to grow
G rass grows back again.

S un beats down
U p in the sky
M any flowers blossom
M any trees have leaves
E veryone has fun
R ain does not fall.

A s leaves fall from trees
U pon a rainy day
T rees go bare
U ntil there is nothing there
M any conkers fall
N othing they're at all.

W inds blow
I ntroducing the snow
N ever hot, always cold
T ime flies by
E mpty trees around
R obins fly around without sound.

James Brown (10)
Five Ways Primary School

WSSA

W is for winter which is freezing cold
S is for springtime, the fun has begun
S is for summer, your paddling pool out
A is for autumn, the leaves begin to fall, it gets darker and darker
                                        as the days go on.

Millie Bell (9)
Five Ways Primary School

The Seasons

The snow falls down
The world is white
And when we awake
What a beautiful sight

Spring is here
But do we know
The trees blossom
The flowers grow
And the birds are singing
To the world below

Summer's here
Once again
Hot sunny days
With hardly any rain
The golden sunshine up so high
Lovely and bright up in the sky

What colour leaves can you see?
Red leaves, yellow leaves, orange and brown
Leaves are blowing off the trees
And slowly falling down.

Danielle Jackson (9)
Five Ways Primary School

Winter

W is for the weather and winds that blow
 I   is for icicles and lots of cold snow
N is for night-time that shortens the day
T   is for trees when the wind makes them sway
E   is for evergreens that grow very tall
R is for the robin so gentle and small
This to me is winter, it can be a wonderful thing
Because when it's all over you then have spring.

Louis McEvoy (9)
Five Ways Primary School

Winter Wonderland

Snowflakes drifting down to the ground
Falling gently without a sound
Santa's here with loads of gifts
That were on our Christmas lists.

Spring
Newly born creatures roam around
Looking for food upon the ground
Lots of wildlife everywhere
Makes you want to stop and stare.

Summer
Golden, lazy, hazy days
The warmth is felt by the sun's rays
Sunbeds out by the pool
The umbrella's shade keeps us cool.

Autumn Leaves
Leaves are rustling on the floor,
The trees are emptying more and more,
Red, brown, yellow and gold
The weather's starting to get cold

Emily O'Sullivan (9)
Five Ways Primary School

Winter

Winter is the season when children get excited
Ice-covered ponds where the ducks skate along
Children play outside with runny noses and rosy-red cheeks
Happily rolling in snow with their bright coloured
Hats, scarves and gloves
Winter brings crisp, dark mornings and freezing cold nights
Evenings are lit by pretty Christmas lights in every window
Our tummies are warmed by lovely roast dinners
Mince pies and the taste of hot chocolate with marshmallows
I love winter because it is when joy and happiness is brought.

Alex Jones (9)
Five Ways Primary School

The Seasons

Starting to get cold
Trees beginning to look bare,
Leaves of red, brown and gold
In September autumn's here.

White blankets everywhere
It starts to get freezing,
Santa brings a teddy bear
In December winter's here.

Flowers start to grow
The sunshine starts to peep,
People start to mow
In March spring is here.

The six weeks holidays have begun
The sun is at its hottest,
People have lots of fun
In June summer's here.

Oliver Clark (9)
Five Ways Primary School

Winter

Cold frosty mornings, Jack Frost's been again
Dad's scraping the car
Icicles are melting drip by drip
Snow beginning to fall on a cold winter's day

Santa's coming soon,
Children are excited building snowmen
Families carol-singing at people's doors
Wrapped up in gloves and scarves

Bang! Bang! Bang! Go the crackers
Families eating turkey around the table
Tinsel decorating the tree
Fairy lights shining bright!

Lauren Parker (9)
Five Ways Primary School

My Favourite Three Seasons

Wonderful Winter!
Snowflakes fall to the ground
Never ever making a sound
Santa comes every December
One time you will always remember!
Winter is here,
So let's give a warming cheer!

Spring is the best!
This is the time when babies are born,
Cute, furry and warm.
The Easter bunny giving you a lucky treat,
When the first lamb starts to bleat!
Warm, hazy days for sleeping in the sun
There's always time for fun!

Summer
Trees are pure green
Always and everywhere to be seen!
Out into the diamond-blue pool,
Where it's icy and cool
In the garden getting a brown tan
Keeping cool with a fan.

Scarlett Baker (9)
Five Ways Primary School

The Winter

When I see the leaves falling
I know that the cold, dark
Winter is coming

The only thing I can see is the time
When Christmas is here

Presents and gifts around the tree
Family and friends are all near

So the cold dark winter is not so bad after all.

Peter Davis (9)
Five Ways Primary School

Winter

It is getting very cold
All the trees look grey
Snow starts to fall
It's winter, hip, hip hooray

Children waking up
Seeing the snow fall
Rolling, rolling, rolling
The snow into a large ball

The snowman is made,
What a beautiful sight
Lots of time left
For a snowball fight.

Excitement is rising for Christmas
The schools close for the break
It is the season of giving
And lots of cakes to make

The snow starts to melt
Christmas has been and gone
It's time to start a new season
Let's hope it's a happy one.

Luke Yeomans-Smith (9)
Five Ways Primary School

Ghosts Of Hallowe'en

Ghosts give you a fright
Ghosts are creepy and white
They can be a scary sight
As they only come out at night

Witches fly in the air
With their dresses ready to scare
Witches fly in the sky
Waiting to make children cry

Hallowe'en is quite fun, but beware they can give you a scare!

Emily Lycett (10)
Five Ways Primary School

Autumn

Colourful crispy leaves falling from the trees,
Many different colours,
Brown, red, orange and green.

Children play with conkers tied to a string,
One, two, three,
What fun this can bring.

Hallowe'en is nearing, Bonfire Night is soon,
Pumpkins, hot dogs, scarves and gloves,
Fireworks fly up to the moon

Farmers harvest all the crops
With tractors on their land,
Children sing and bring their gifts
To give a helping hand.

Autumn is enjoyable for all of us to see,
But wrap up warm, prepare yourself,
As winter follows me!

Emily Bradburn (9)
Five Ways Primary School

Seasons

The strong wind blows
The leaves from the trees
Red, brown and gold are the colour of the leaves
As Jack Frost returns to turn on the freeze
The snow clouds fall and cover the floor
As green grass grows new lambs are born!
The tulips and daffodils return at dawn
As the days grow long
The sun shines down strong
There's fruit on the trees
And honey from the bees
Another year has passed
But it won't be the last.

Jack Garner (9)
Five Ways Primary School

Spring's The Season

Baby animals sitting in the grass
It's getting warmer at last
There's bulbs and flowers
And April showers
Don't you love the spring?

The Easter bunny is coming soon
Now's the time to sing a tune
To celebrate the chocolate treats
Good children get they know nothing beats
The spring

The new leaves are sprouting on the trees
The clocks go forward, get ready to tease
April Fool's here we can play a trick
I know what season to pick
Cos I love the spring!

Eleanor Dewsbury (10)
Five Ways Primary School

Winter

Wintertime is here again
With cold days and nights
And bright fairy lights
The snow comes tumbling down

We all run out and throw about
The snow upon the ground
I hear the crunching sound beneath my feet
I realise it's time for a cosy retreat

I lie in bed
Thoughts in my head
As I snuggle down in my bed
I drift into a dreamy sleep
Of Christmas times I'd like to keep.

Ryan Higginson (11)
Five Ways Primary School

The Seasons

Three hundred and sixty-five days,
Big Ben chiming to the start of the year,
Fifty-two weeks, happiness and sadness,
New Year's Eve, friends and families,
Seasons changing, new things happening,
Planets revolving, children growing.

Winter fun, snowmen jolly,
Snowflakes falling, bare trees blowing,
Gusty wind and heavy snow,
Hats and scarves, warming toes,
Santa and his reindeer, ice skating on lakes,
Dark nights and short days, hard frozen earth.

Spring joy and Easter bunnies,
Soft squidgy moss, trees growing their leaves,
Flowers are blooming, chocolate and children,
April showers and clocks going forwards,
Bright green grass and high shining rainbows,
Baby animals playing, snowdrops and daffodils.

Summer smiles, camping with cubs,
Sun shining down and people getting tans,
Diving and surfing and outdoor activities,
Heat waves rising and the sea getting full,
Long lazy days, *no more school!*
Paddling in the pool and people on planes.

Autumn frolics and falling leaves,
Red and brown colours everywhere to be seen,
Clocks going backwards and the harvest gathered in,
People trick and treating, smiling pumpkins in windows,
Squirrels gathering nuts in the golden reflecting sun,
Splashing in puddles with hard breezes blowing.

Thomas Birch (9)
Five Ways Primary School

All Of The Seasons

Spring
Spring has arrived so have all the flowers and friends,
New baby lambs and birds that sing,
Trees get their leaves all big and green,
Is spring your favourite season?

Summer
Summer has begun the sun shines down,
It brings sunbathing, holidays and swimming in your pool,
No school and ice cream to keep us cool,
Is summer your favourite season?

Autumn
The weather cools down, trees are getting bare,
Gold, brown and leaves floating everywhere,
Conkers and acorns lying to be found,
Is autumn your favourite season?

Winter
Now it is cold as cold as can be,
Having the fun through throwing snowballs at me,
Sleighing down hills with icicles on trees,
Is winter your favourite season?

Jack Dace (9)
Five Ways Primary School

Autumn Is Here

Autumn is coming
Lots of fun
Crispy leaves have just fallen
Bright colours of orange and red
I love to throw the leaves around my head
As I walk through the street
The leaves crunch beneath my feet
As the wind blows the leaves away
I say, 'Hey come back, I want to play.'

Matthew Joyce (9)
Five Ways Primary School

Seasons

The dark days lighten
The bright flowers grow
The harsh winter's over
Spring starts to show

The trees have blossomed
The blazing sun
Spring's over
Summer's begun

The hot weather's cooling
The crispy brown leaves fall
Autumn's forming
The wind gives a great call

The soft rain's frozen
Crystal icicles hang
The floor is white
Winter's sang.

Andy Spurr (9)
Five Ways Primary School

Seasons

Seasons are great
You can play with your mates
Summer comes hot
Autumn leaves drop
Thunder goes *pop*
Winter is so cold
Leaves start to mould
Nights go dark
Dogs start to bark
We all go to bed
Everything goes dead
The seasons are led.

Kieran Meredith (9)
Five Ways Primary School

Bubblegum

Rip it out the packet
Then stuff it all in
Chew it like you mean it
With an enormous grin

Wrap it around your tongue
And see how it grows
You'll be running out of breath
Before your tiredness shows

A huge ball of sugar
Is fizzing around your lips
A sticky gooey mess, is on your fingertips

Then out comes the hand
Like a sharp knitting pin
It punctures the thin sweet
That was tickling on your chin

The precious layer bursts
And is glued to your cheeks
Your pleasure has now ended
You wish you had more *sweets!*

Shannon David (10)
Five Ways Primary School

I Long For Winter

Autumn is coming, the weather is turning cold
The trees are shedding their leaves all turning red and gold
Time has come to dress up warm
To shelter from the storm
With temperatures low
I long for winter, to play in the snow.

Edward Evans (9)
Five Ways Primary School

A Pocketful Of Rhyme

New buds are sprouting
Blossom is coming
Get out your wellies and brollies too
Splashing in puddles is great fun for you

The sky is blue
The sun is shining
The birds are singing
The schools are ending

New term is starting
Schools are opening
Leaves are changing colour
Green, brown, and red

The snow is falling
Christmas is near
A new year is coming
More school is near.

Ben Watson (10)
Five Ways Primary School

Wintertime

Cold in the morning
Cold at night
Cold in our beds
So snuggle up tight

Ice on the pavement
Frost in the air
Don't run too fast
You'd better take care

Christmas is coming
Get out your tree
Presents all round
As far as you can see.

Bradley Woodhouse (9)
Five Ways Primary School

Seasons

Winter is snowy and very cold
Winter is fine playing out in the cold
The days are short and nights are long
But it's good when Santa comes along

Hooray, spring is here, the days are getting warmer
Newborn lambs are playing in the field
Daffodils are growing in grassy parts of the wood
I like spring because summer is near

Great! Summer is here, everybody is playing
Blue skies are lovely, the sun is shining
School is over, holidays are here
Summer is great, surfing on the waves.

Autumn has arrived, beautiful coloured leaves are on the ground
Trees are bare; it is getting cold
Geese fly all the way to Canada
Before we know it, winter is here.

Sam Nutting (9)
Five Ways Primary School

Snow

It's snowing outside,
Hooray, hooray,
It's white all over,
There'll be no school today!

The wind is blowing,
The flakes swirl all around,
They float so softly
Upon the crisp, crunchy ground

The sky is so heavy,
There's more snow to come,
It's so chilly outside,
Winter has finally begun.

Joe Emery (9)
Five Ways Primary School

Autumn To Winter

As the leaves turn
From green to golden-yellow
As the nights turn
From brightness to darkness
Summer ends and autumn begins

The children in their welly boots
Playing with the leaves
The children with their hats and gloves
Throwing their sticks to get the conkers
Yes, autumn has begun

The wet leaves abandoned on the ground
The trees stand tall with bare twigs
Morning starts with a frosty glaze
Icy patches appear on the ground
Autumn ends, winter begins.

The children on their sleighs
Playing in the snow
Houses all lit up and decorated
Presents wrapped with ribbon under the Christmas tree
Yes, winter has begun.

Adam Tolladay (9)
Five Ways Primary School

Summer

School has finished, hip hip hooray
It's time to go out and play
People go on holidays, away from wet and windy days
The beach is a fun place to play
Jump about it's your holiday
Sand in your hair
Sand in your toes
Look how nice that sandcastle glows
The sun is hot, you feel it burning on your skin
Go into the sea and watch everyone grin.

Lauren Tonks (9)
Five Ways Primary School

Seasons All Through The Year

Winter is cold and full of snow
The snowmen I build have an icy glow,
It's also the time of Christmas cheer,
That's why winter is my favourite time of year.

Spring is when the flowers start to grow,
And little lambs jump to and fro,
In April we get showery weather,
And splash in puddles together.

Summer is usually very hot,
We go to the beach and play a lot,
We eat ice creams and splash in the sea,
And then it's home, in time for tea.

Autumn is when the leaves fall down,
And swirl around about the town,
Squirrels like to play together,
And gather nuts for the cold weather.

Sophie Woodall (10)
Five Ways Primary School

A Whole Year

January, hooray! It's New Year,
But I was cold through to February and March,
Till the crocuses popped up their heads
And I ate Easter eggs in April
May passed and Father's Day arrived
The sun is hot in July and August
The leaves are falling, autumn is beginning
The ghosts and ghouls have arrived it's Hallowe'en
The bonfire is lit, Catherine wheels are spinning
Twirling and turning, twisting and banging,
It's cold, colder, freezing, snowing
Christmas is here - Santa's arrived.

Gabrielle Purshouse (9)
Five Ways Primary School

Seasons

This is the time lambs are born
Mad March hares on the lawn
This is the time chicks are found
Waddling around on the ground

This is the time for sandcastles on the beach
Daddy's no good, time to teach
This is the time to play in the park
Having lots of fun until it goes dark

This is the time that leaves turn gold
Yellow, orange, red, brown and bold.
This is the time I go play,
Kicking leaves for the rest of the day.

This is the time for snow to fall,
Cold, wet and frosty for all,
This is the time for fog and cold air,
Nobody cares, it's Christmas Fayre.

Charlotte Brindley (9)
Five Ways Primary School

Winter Poem

I woke up this morning
Looked out of my window
The snow was falling
Hooray, winter is dawning

I rushed to put on my warm clothes
To get a carrot for my snowman's nose
I ran outside as fast as I could
To build a snowman no one else would

I rolled a ball of snow for my snowman's head
Then my sister got out of bed!
We rolled a ball of snow for his body
Then he really began to look like somebody
Our creation was done and now we can have some fun.

Elliot Woolley (10)
Five Ways Primary School

A Poem About Seasons

Spring is here, new life is to be found,
Fluffy white lambs are born to leap around,
Birds tweet and sing, what a lovely sound,
Flowers are growing from beneath the ground.

Summer shines through the hot, blazing sun,
Play parks are full of children,
Ice creams melting, oh what fun!
I love the summer, it's simply the best.

Autumn is here the ground is full of leaves
Rolling mists across fields go on forever,
Golds, reds and browns are the colours of the trees,
Collecting brown conkers to hit together.

Winter colds send shivers down my spine,
Pretty snowflakes fall through the misty skies,
Harry the hedgehog hibernating, he'll be fine
Father Christmas, delivered his presents,
It's time to fly!

Amy Grace Baker (9)
Five Ways Primary School

My Sister

I have a baby sister who really is quite sweet
But all she seems to do all day
Is eat, play and sleep

She giggles and she gurgles and makes lots of funny noise
And when I want to play alone she pinches all my toys

She crawls around on hands and knees it really is quite strange
'Cause although she's the one that makes all the mess
I still get the blame

When my sister is ready for bed she rubs her sleepy eyes
She snuggles down and has her milk
And then we all say goodnight.

Ashley Sumner (10)
Five Ways Primary School

Seasons In Life

My ice cream is melting
It's just that time of year
When days are hot, the air is warm
I can sense it on my face.

Today I need my coat on
It's as cold as cold can be
The warmth has gone along with the sun
It's that Christmas time of year.

This season is the start for some little newborn lambs,
It's the start of the year when the exciting part comes,
Along with the sun.

It's nearly the end of the year after,
Warmth from the sun,
We start putting our coats on,
Leaves fall off the trees and cold winds,
Blow and start to get stronger.

Rebecca Purchase (10)
Five Ways Primary School

My Rabbit Fluffy

I have got a rabbit called Fluffy
Who is sometimes a little bit scruffy
He lies to eat hay and play all day
And he likes to drink plenty of water
He lies in the sun having lots of fun
And sometimes digs holes in our garden
He likes to play football and push it around
But he never ever makes a sound
He likes to eat carrots
Chomp, chomp, chomp
But his favourite treat is Dad's favourite plant
But we don't mind because
We love him so much.

Chantelle Burton (10)
Five Ways Primary School

Seasons All Through The Year

The Winter
The snow is crispy under your feet
The snow is falling from the sky
You can see it if you look up high

The Spring
Spring is in the air
There are shoots everywhere
The plants are growing one by one
The crispy leaves are gone, gone, gone!

The Summer
Summer is hot once again,
The birds are singing again and again

The Autumn
Autumn is getting colder and colder
Winter is coming and the people are
Getting bitter and bitter.

Ryan Phillips (9)
Five Ways Primary School

My Rabbit Snoopy

I've got a rabbit called Snoopy
I think he's very loopy
He's big, fluffy and grey
In the morning I let him out to play
Now all our bright green grass has gone
So now we're left with none
His nose is very twitchy
I wonder if it's itchy
His ears are very floppy
That's probably why he's so hoppy
He bounces here and there
But this rabbit needs a lot of care.

Ryan Arnold (10)
Five Ways Primary School

Seasons

Spring is newborn lambs and chicks
The birds are making their nests with sticks
The buds on the trees are starting to grow
We have now seen the last of the snow

Summer is full of fun
We run outside in the sun
Every year we go on holiday
To the sand and sea we go and play

Autumn is falling leaves
Red, yellow, brown and green
All about upon the ground
You can see lots of mounds

Winter is full of fun
In the snow we jump and run
In December it's Christmas time
Santa brings gifts and drinks some wine.

James Statham (9)
Five Ways Primary School

Summer

The sun is shining in the sky
Kites are flying way up high

Children playing hand in hand
Waves crashing on the sand

Boats are sailing out to sea
Busy working the bumblebee

Smell the hot dogs on the van
Buy an ice cream from the man

People bathing on the sand
Bodies burning and getting tanned.

Matthew Jones (9)
Five Ways Primary School

My Mate

My pet is a pony,
He keeps me from getting lonely,
His name is Roger,
He's quick like the Artful Dodger.

When in the stable,
If he's able,
He does nothing all day,
But eats plenty of hay.

In the field he enjoys green grass,
He has a bridle of leather and brass,
A saddle so comfy,
When riding Roger he's never grumpy.

He's fast like a black panther cat,
He likes a friendly pat,
Roger's my mate,
And I think he's great.

Jonathan Whitbread (10)
Five Ways Primary School

Bert

There was a man called Bert
Who slipped on some leaves in the dirt
He said, 'Cor blimey,
The leaves are all slimy
I'm glad I did not fall and get hurt.'

Along came winter, all snowy and cold
Bert felt the chill, because he was old,
He wrapped up snugly to keep himself warm
He stayed indoors, away from harm
'I can't wait for spring and the sun shining gold.'

James Evans (9)
Five Ways Primary School

My Best Friend

I had a friend called Jay,
We would play and play all day,
Every day he used to say,
'Let's play, let's play.'

But then one day came a very cold day,
So I couldn't play with Jay,
I forgot when he used to say,
'Let's play, let's play.'

One day I went on holiday,
But I didn't go with Jay,
I forgot when he used to say,
'Let's play, let's play.'

Then one day I was able to play
With my best friend Jay,
But he didn't say what he used to say,
He said, 'Hooray, hooray!'

Rachael Collins (10)
Five Ways Primary School

Autumn Is A Wonderful Thing

Autumn is a wonderful thing
It's dark in the morning when the birds start to sing
You don't hear much when autumn is here
But mostly you see the deer
And two minutes later, Santa is here
After that, presents appear
Once again snowmen are built.

Summer is a wonderful thing
And light in the morning when the bells start to ring
You hear lots of fun when summer has begun
Children playing, singing and dancing
Laughing with laughter.

Kelly Pugh (9)
Five Ways Primary School

Football

I like football, I like fun,
When I kick the ball using my boot,
I see the ball round and hard,
Hit the goalie as I shoot.

I like football, I like fun,
When I head the ball as it hits the back of the net,
I feel great and forget the pain in my head.

I like football, I like fun
As I run around the pitch,
I sometimes fall on my bum,
But when I score I forget my bum is numb.

I like football, I like fun,
My favourite team is Chelsea
Who can always beat Man U,
Man U play in red, Chelsea play in blue,
This is my favourite colour and it should be for you!

Calum Gallier (10)
Five Ways Primary School

The Tree

In spring the tree will get buds of all sorts like colourful jelly babies
And little leaves like soft sweet grapes

In summer the tree will display
Its bright green beautiful leaves like a peacock

In autumn the tree will have gold, red and brown
Beautiful leaves that fall to the ground
And crunch like chocolate wrappers

In winter the tree will have lost all the leaves
Not one to be found but will still have the beauty
Of the frost as the sun gazes on it
That is the story of the tree through the seasons.

Jack Terry (9)
Five Ways Primary School

Sports

I like sports
My favourite sport is hockey
But I really like football
And tag rugby

I play football for the school
On Wednesdays it's really fun
Especially when I get dirty
It's really fun

I wish I could play hockey out of school
But I can't, there's nowhere to go
It's really fun

I like to play tag rugby
I play for the school
So does my brother
It's really fun.

Lucy Gladston (11)
Five Ways Primary School

Winter

Winter air hits your face and freezes your nose
Winter is hearing laughter as children play in the snow
Winter is very cold and icy
Winter is exciting, Christmas is coming
Winter freezes the ponds and the ducks can't swim
Winter gets dark at 5pm and is dark still in the morning
Winter makes icicles that are very sharp
Winter can be lots of fun.

Tom Showell (9)
Five Ways Primary School

Seasons

In Autumn
The ground is as orange as fire
Mum has to clean up
But the next day the pile is higher

In Summer
The sun is as hot as flames
The children buy water bombs
And play water games.

In Winter
All the cold snow drops
All the children have snowball fights
And there are no crops

In Spring
The birds sing happy songs
Blossom's on the tree
And the nights get long.

Harry Clinton (10)
Five Ways Primary School

Seasons

In the wintertime we go walking in fields of snow
Autumn is cold, crispy too
I like it a lot hope you do too
Summer's hot I like it a lot
Pools and ice creams
Also the beautiful streams
Spring is hot, cold too
I don't like it much, but you might do.

Matt Olorenshaw (10)
Five Ways Primary School

The Winter Poem

The nights are dark
The weather cold
We sit by the fire
To keep ourselves warm
We play games
To have fun
We snuggle together
And think of warmer weather
When we go out
We wrap up warm
Playing together
Till it turns to dusk
Looking through
The windows
Waiting for
Snow to fall
Dreaming of a
Time when
Fun will be
Had by all
With Christmas
Lights twinkling
Presents by the tree
Knowing Santa's on his way
Is fun for you and me.

Owen Jenkinson (9)
Five Ways Primary School

Winter Is Cold

Winter is cold, but I don't care
I look out the window and there's snow everywhere.
There's plenty for us to play and do
I put on my gloves and hat and scarf too.
Christmas is coming, people have smiles
If you be good you will have toys in piles!

Adam Scargill (9)
Five Ways Primary School

The Haunted Window

I looked through the window
What did I see?
A fearsome ghoul
Looking at me!
With big gloomy eyes
A big red cap
With a screech and a cackle
That sounds like rap

I looked through the window
What did I see?
A vicious old witch
Scowling at me!
A wart on her nose
A green hooked chin
An uneven smile
Showing a toothless grin.

I looked through the window,
What did I see?
A bloodthirsty vampire
Glaring at me!
With needle-sharp fangs
And breath like Hell
Two orb-like eyes
And a pungent smell.

Matthew Round (10)
Five Ways Primary School

My Day Of Fun!

S un is up in the bright blue sky
U nbreaking sunshine in which we lie
M elting ice creams and lollipops
M ini skirts and summer tops
E njoying splashing in the pool
R eally happy, got no school!

Danielle Samson (9)
Five Ways Primary School

Magical Seasons

Summer

Bright sun shining on my back,
Barbecues lighting up my face,
Young children splashing in the pool,
Ice creams making everyone cool,
Holidays taken by the sea,
Summer is the best time for me.

Winter

Nose and fingers tingling,
Woolly hats and gloves keeping me warm,
Walking to school slipping and skating on ice,
Children having snow fights,
Hear the cracking of Christmas crackers,
Winter is magical for me.

Megan Atkinson (9)
Five Ways Primary School

My Dog McKenzie

When I first saw McKenzie
I could tell he was mad
And I could tell he was a lad
His fur was the colour of a milk chocolate bar
I could tell he was the right dog for me
I couldn't wait for my friends to see him
When we got home he was a bit scared
I gave him lots of hugs and cuddles
And he settled down to sleep
He slept for most of the day
So we couldn't hear a peep
He is very important to our family
In lots of ways
McKenzie is my new lifelong friend.

Hannah Lote (10)
Five Ways Primary School

Fun

Fun is a warm crisp orange
like a warm hot fire that warms everybody up.
It tastes like pink sherbet fizzing away in your mouth.
It smells like warm chocolate melting in your mouth.
Fun sounds like loud children playing in the playground.
It reminds me of when I was a young boy
and I was having fun with my friends.
It feels like you are riding a roller coaster at high speed.

Michael McGann (10)
Hayes Meadow Primary School

Sadness

Sadness is the colour of light blue on a foggy day
It smells like water-filled tears dripping down your face
It tastes like sweet tangy chocolate orange
It sounds like your hamster running on the wheel
It feels like you're all alone with no one there
It reminds you of the day someone in your family died
It looks like your friend has gone to another friend.

Courtney Stockle
Hayes Meadow Primary School

Valentine's Day

The pink world is full of love and everyone likes each other
The sweet scent and raspberry taste makes every girl and boy happy
Birds cheep and sing in the lovely spring place
You can hear harps everywhere
And you feel so soft in the morning

And that's the beauty of Valentine's Day.

Mia Parry
Hayes Meadow Primary School

Love

Love is like a light pink fluffy cushion that you want to cuddle
It tastes like a soft marshmallow that you want to fall on
It smells like a bottle of expensive perfume
It sounds like a harp floating in the breeze
It feels like a soft fluffy cloud that you want to fall asleep on
It reminds me of a pink limo with pink fluffy interior
It looks like a pink love heart that you want to cuddle.

Megan McMeel
Hayes Meadow Primary School

Fun

Fun is a warm crisp orange
Like a warm hot fire that everybody likes at night
Fun tastes like pink fuzzy sherbet in your mouth
Fun sounds like laughing at a funfair
Fun smells like delicious chocolate melting in your mouth
Fun looks like all the little children playing on the rides
Fun feels like playing football on a hot summer's day
Fun is *great!*

Callum McComisky (9)
Hayes Meadow Primary School

Sadness

Sadness is dark grey like a rusty old shed
Sadness tastes like mouldy bread
Sadness smells like green water in the sewer
Sadness sounds like loneliness when no one likes you
Sadness reminds me of when I'm upset
Sadness looks like a dark lonely house that's crumbling to the floor.

Josef Bogunovic (10)
Hayes Meadow Primary School

Love Is For Everyone

Love is a delicate red that comes from your heart
Love is what you share with the girl of your dreams
Love can break your heart into many pieces
Love will always give you your first kiss
Love is for roses and candles with expensive French wine in an
expensive restaurant
Love will always make you feel happy
At last love could change you into a caring person.

Mason Joyce (11)
Hayes Meadow Primary School

Love

Love is red like a love heart
It feels like a big red silky cushion
It smells like a fresh bowl of fruit
It sounds like your heart is pounding
It tastes like some bars of chocolate melting onto a box of
fresh strawberries
It reminds me of some heart-shaped clouds
It looks like a red silky heart-shaped tree.

Chloe Andrea
Hayes Meadow Primary School

Sadness

Sadness is dark blue like the sun going down
Sadness hurts but it still makes you frown
It feels like your friend has ditched you and no one's around
Sadness is for people who sit alone
Sadness is an emotion that can be worked out.

Joshua Duffy
Hayes Meadow Primary School

Love

Love is bright and cheerful pinks and red like the colour of hearts from
a husband to his wife.
Love tastes like fresh, succulent strawberries.
Love smells like a romantic pudding at a famous restaurant.
Love sounds like expensive red wine sloshing into tall glasses.
Love looks like diamond-shaped roses in an expensive vase straight
from your heart!

I think of love as romantic!

Emily Fisher
Hayes Meadow Primary School

Fun

Fun is bright yellow like the gleaming sun
Fun smells like candyfloss at the fairground
Fun feels like you're on top of the world
Fun sounds like a DJ blasting his music
Fun looks like you're on top of a roller coaster waiting to drop
Fun tastes like a chocolate fountain
Fun reminds me of a hen night.

Megan Young (9)
Hayes Meadow Primary School

Anger

Anger is a deep dark red like when a volcano is erupting
It feels like your hands are on fire
It sounds like a bomb blowing up in Iraq
It reminds me of World War II when the massive guns are shooting
It tastes like spicy sauce burning your tongue
It smells like smoke when the house is burning down.

Joshua Cornes (9)
Hayes Meadow Primary School

Happiness

Happiness is like a bright sparkling yellow
that flows all around you.

Happiness tastes like a simple, soft, squashy
sweet that weakens in your mouth.

Happiness smells like a light red strawberry rose
that falls to pieces every time you touch it.

Happiness sounds like birds chirping in
the bright green trees.

Happiness feels like a hamster running
in your hand.

Happiness reminds me of love because
it makes people feel happy.

Happiness looks like trees blowing calmly
in the distance.

Ben Yates
Hayes Meadow Primary School

Happiness

Happiness is bright and cheerful
It is jolly
It is a bright lemon
Happiness is a bunch of fun

It smells like emerald-green grass
With drops of glittering dew
Happiness is a twinkling view
Like water, nice and blue

It looks like joy
With skies of light blue
Happiness is like playing with toys
Happiness is a great entertainment.

Kerry Baily (10)
Hayes Meadow Primary School

A Footballer

A footballer is claret and blue
He is wintertime
He is a football match
He is rainy
He wears a football kit
He is a football stadium
He is 'Match of the Day'
He is a pizza.

Daniel Kinsella (8)
Lichfield Cathedral School

Octopoem

A horse is boy
She is the summertime
In a field
Hot and sunny
A shiny leather saddle
A large bucket of water
How to look after horses
Oats and carrots.

Annabel Forrest-King (8)
Lichfield Cathedral School

Fairy

A fairy is pink
She is summertime
In a fairy bedroom
She is sunny
A glittering shimmery dress
On her light
Tinkerbell
Sugary cake.

Jessica Shaw (8)
Lichfield Cathedral School

Oceans

Deep blue oceans
Sea creatures live there
Sharks lurking
Dolphins jumping
Chasing things for the fun

The big blue whale
With his tail in the air
Catching krill for his tea
I wish this was me

A gang of mackerel shoot by
Flashing their tummies in the evening sky
Dolphins chasing
For it is time to eat

The great white shark
With his long sharp teeth
Fills me with fear
As he swims near

Seals playing on the beach
Here comes a whale
Little seals watch out
Because this killer is about

Where the clowns live
Over by the reef
But at night
Who is the chief?

The crabs are scavenging
By the shallow rocks
But this is where the fishermen
Have put their pots.

Finley Saunders (8)
Lichfield Cathedral School

Shopping

Shopping, shopping I go twice a week
I think shopping is very bleak
I don't like shopping one tiny bit!
The supermarket makes me feel rather sick
The only kind of shopping I really like is for clothes
Or for a bike . . .

Food shopping is not so bad now
Because everything is in one shop
Look over there, some clothes and bikes
That's what I really like!

Beth Jacob (8)
Lichfield Cathedral School

I Can . . .

I can jump higher than a bouncing kangaroo
I can run faster than a cheetah, it's true
I can think quicker than a wise old owl
I can dry my hands slower on a tissue than a towel
I can grow faster than a flower in May
I can eat quicker than a horse eating hay
I can throw further than an athlete in the Olympics
I can lick quicker than a dog that does sloppy licks
I can fly higher than a bird in the sky
I have more meat than a big meat pie.

Natasha Rowland-Lovett (9)
Lichfield Cathedral School

I Can

I can think quicker than a wise old owl
I can scream louder than wolves who howl
I can jog speedier than a rocket blaster
I can munch quicker than a horse who eats pasta.

Fern Bradley (8)
Lichfield Cathedral School

The World

The world has healthy people and they have nice homes
Our world has poor and unhealthy people that don't have nice homes

In our world there are animals that are in danger

In our world some children go to school
and some children don't go to school

On our world we have not a lot of forest
They have been chopped down to make new roads

In our oceans we have beautiful corals and fish
In our oceans we have poisons from factories that kill our fish

In our skies we have fluffy white clouds
And singing birds

In our skies we have gasses from cars that change our weather.

Chloe Newton (8)
Lichfield Cathedral School

Sports

Uni hockey, my brothers are jockeys
Table tennis, I'm a menace
I am swimming and I am winning
While I'm running I get cunning

In cricket I get a wicket
In long jump I land with a bump
When playing soccer I dribble the ball and kick it against the wall
When I am playing lacrosse I slip on the moss

In the game of bowls I must avoid any holes
When I go sailing if I capsize I start wailing
My golf swing makes me want to sing.

Eleanor Proudlove (9)
Lichfield Cathedral School

Sonny Jim

Once there was a little robin
His name was Sonny Jim
He stood on the side of the bird bath
And then he fell in.

He flipped, he flapped
He flapped, he flipped
Until his wings were dry
He took a great big jump
And flew high into the sky.

My daddy stood in the garden
With a catapult
He shot at Sonny Jim
Who did a somersault.

Molly Beharrell (9)
Lichfield Cathedral School

Red Eyes

Some cats eat cat food
Some cats eat fish
But no, my cat eats . . .
Humans!

Some cats have blue eyes
Some cats have green eyes
But no, my cat has . . .
Red eyes!

Could you imagine a cat with red eyes
Who eats humans for tea?
Would you like
To meet him?

Harry Whiting (9)
Lichfield Cathedral School

Me

I can tame a two-headed dog
I cam jump on a moving log
I am sillier than a stupid clown
I can travel to an Indian town
I can buzz more than a bee
I can balance on one knee
I can build a card out of log
I can see right through the fog
Nothing is heavy for me
I can shout louder than my friend Lee
I can somersault in my house
I can keep a four-headed mouse.

Nicholas Kearns (8)
Lichfield Cathedral School

The Pig

The pig is pink
He likes the summertime
He lives on a farm
He is sunny
He has a warm woolly cloak
A shiny trough
Babe
Crispy bacon!

Andrew Murphy (7)
Lichfield Cathedral School

Magic Cat - Haiku

I am magic cat
I pounce, purr, scratch and attack
Invisible me.

Isabella James (8)
Lichfield Cathedral School

Twists And Turns

One observant old orange ostrich
Two terrible tame trout
Three thirsty thriving tortoises
Four funky fruity funny birds
Five frightened fine phoney sick thimbles
Six snacking spying snakes
Seven snowy scary sea lions
Eight eager eels eating electric eels
Nine neat neighbours
Ten tiny thinking tortoises.

Hannah Lawson (7)
Lichfield Cathedral School

Tongue Twister

One fish finger flapping about
Two ticking tortoise talking
Three frog-talking teachers
Four fish fishing about
Five fancy flying flapping fish fingers
Six singing sausages
Seven sitting singing Simpsons
Eight hugging hungry hammers
Nine nipping naughty newts
Ten tickling tortoises.

Minnie Butlin (7)
Lichfield Cathedral School

Fun

Fun is as yellow as the sun
It sounds like a laughing sound
It tastes sweet and it smells real good
It feels like tickles on my skin
It makes me happy when I have fun.

Archie Hulse (7)
Lichfield Cathedral School

Friendship

Friendship is as white as a cloud
It sounds like the wind
And it tastes like chocolate cake
Friendship smells like roses
It looks like snow
And it feels like a soft wind blowing in my hair
Friendship is as loving as home
It's like putting on a pair of comfy slippers
And floating off to bed
Friendship is forever
And I hope it never ends.

Francesca York (7)
Lichfield Cathedral School

Hallowe'en

Hallowe'en, Hallowe'en
Ghostly ghouls and white ghosts
Cauldrons and candy on posts
Toffee apples and pumpkins
Look scared!
Vampire bats and axemen
Jack o' lanterns and Captain Hook
Oh, just costume turn on the light
'Argh!'
It's not over yet!

Maxim Hibbs (8)
Lichfield Cathedral School

Stupidity

Stupidity is purple
It tastes like rotten cabbage
Sounds like a mini frog
It feels like a biscuit gone wrong.

Simon Ashwood (7)
Lichfield Cathedral School

A Cat Has What?

A cat has fur
A cat has a tail
A cat has legs
And a cat has a head

A cat has eyes
A cat has paws
And a cat has a voice that says, 'Time for food,
Lovely food!'

The food is chicken
The food is pork
The food is fish
The food is tuna
Only kidding it's liver
I wait at the doorstep at 12 o'clock waiting and
Waiting forever and a day.

Molly Dell (9)
Lichfield Cathedral School

The Selfish Bully

The selfish bully
Mean and popular

Naughty and cruel
Such a fool

So mean to John
So mean to Joshua

But poor old John
Left out and sad

So upset that he
Called his dad.

Robert McIntosh (8)
Lichfield Cathedral School

Bully, Oh Bully

Sometimes I can go off in a mood
They say I'm really rude

But I have to think
Whether I want to be poured with ink

Or to try
Have a go at using my goodness

But being good means being kind and helpful
I suppose seeing me good, would be a change

It might be fun

But if they try to bully me
Then I would have to run.

Victoria Gough (8)
Lichfield Cathedral School

Purr Cat

Cats go to sleep
   When the sofa is neat
      They get out at night
         For some fish and chips.

      Cats and mice would be nice
         Play with wool in the lounge
            Unwinding it round and round
            On the floor.

         Scratching the wallpaper
           And clawing at the door
           Making a loud
              Purr, purr
                Purr . . .

James Lloyd (9)
Lichfield Cathedral School

Animals In The Wild

Slithering, sliding, slippery snakes
All red and black, catch mice and rats
Rattling, poisonous, hissing, biting
That is what they do in the wild

Hairy, hectic gorillas and apes
Swing through the air from branch to branch
Gliding, swooping, laughing, chattering
That is what they do in the wild

Enormous elephants wrinkly grey
Splashing with water as they play
Trumpeting, thundering, gulping, washing
That is what they do in the wild

Snapping alligators, creeping crocs
Watching suspiciously, feeling for prey
Gnarling, snarling, jagged teeth, ripping
That is what they do in the wild

Giraffe, long and lean, tall and elegant
Galloping free across the dry land
Munching, running, sometimes cunning
That is what they do in the wild.

Madeleine Sanders (8)
Lichfield Cathedral School

Birthdays

It is my birthday today
I invite my friends to play
I open my presents and find a game
A CD, a car and a plane
I feel excited that it is my birthday
I will play with my toys all day.

William Harvey (8)
Lichfield Cathedral School

Space

Space, space, wonderful space
The moon, the stars and of course Mars
Pluto, Saturn, Uranus, Venus and all the others
Bad, bad black holes sucks the light in the hole
The sun goes down, the moon comes up
Rockets take off into the air flying high into space
Onto Jupiter the biggest planet
My favourite planet Jupiter big and scary and the red dot big
So that's what I like about space!

Henry Southan (8)
Lichfield Cathedral School

Hallowe'en

Today it is Hallowe'en so let's make something nice to eat
Pizza with cobwebs on it with spiders falling on your food
Let's have a fancy dress party
I will be the fanciest one, I will win
Then I will win Crackpot's competition
Then my brother will take me home
And I will dream about what I did
And fall asleep.

Olivia Thackray (8)
Lichfield Cathedral School

Anger!

The robot's eyes are as red as blood
The drum beats *thump, thump, thump*
Hot chillies burn in my mouth
The smell of fire rising in the air
Darkness surrounds me
It feels hard and cold in my heart
That's what I think anger is.

Elliott Manley (7)
Lichfield Cathedral School

Hallowe'en

The moon is shining in the sky
While vampire bats circle by
Haunted house full of cobwebs
With great big spiders hanging down!
Playing games in the street
Apple bobbing, trick or treat?
Lots of witches whizzing by
Followed by the ghosts that cry
Glowing pumpkins all around
Flickering in the wind
Wolves howling all night long
Oh, I hope it's only Hallowe'en.

Lottie Pike (8)
Lichfield Cathedral School

Hallowe'en

Spooks are coming
Hallowe'en is here
Children dressing up to be the spooks
Some as witches, all in black
Long green hair and pointed hats
Children knocking on front doors
The question is to 'trick or treat?'
Smiling faces as the sweets pile up
Mischievous fun when they deal a trick
Pumpkins glowing in the windows
Twinkling stars.

Nicole Higgins (8)
Lichfield Cathedral School

Outrageous Animals

One old, odd, orange, outrageous ostrich
Two terrible, talented, tame, toxic tree-frogs
Three thin, thankful, thoughtful thrushes
Four fast, famous , fat, fashionable foxes
Five fancy, fat, feathered female falcons
Six sad, skinny, secret, shy sheep
Seven savage, scary, serious, sharp sharks
Eight elderly, English, evil elephants
Nine nice, neat, new, noble newts
Ten tall, talented, toy teddy bears.

Alex Wakefield (8)
Lichfield Cathedral School

Outrageous Animals

One old, odd, orange, outrageous ostrich
Two terrible, tame, toxic tree-frogs
Three thin, thankfully famous, thinking tortoises
Four flying, freckled, funky, furred frogs
Five fancy, flapping, fantastic firebirds
Six sad, skinny, swimming sweets
Seven small, sparkling slugs
Eight exciting, English elephants
Nine nasty, naughty, nutty newts
Ten tiny, tuna-thin Thunderbirds.

Richard Chapman (7)
Lichfield Cathedral School

Hallowe'en

Hallowe'en is every year
Today is Hallowe'en
I love Hallowe'en
I like to dress up

Today is Hallowe'en
We get to go trick or treating
It is very dark
As we look up to the starry night

Hallowe'en is over
I feel very sad
I can't wait until next year
To go trick or treating again.

Siobhan Carlin (8)
Lichfield Cathedral School

Cool Cat!

One old orange observant ostrich
Two teachers in trousers
Three Thursday thrushes
Four fast female flowers
Five flying farm-animal fish
Six sad swimming sharks
Seven sharp sky swordfish
Eight English elderly elephants
Nine new nice nutty newts.

Oliver Chatham (8)
Lichfield Cathedral School

Ten Terrible Tongue Twisters

One odd old orange owl
Two tall tame tickled termites
Three thunderous thunderstorms
Four fast famous farm animals
Five fantastic freckled fish
Six savage silver sheep
Seven serious silver sharks
Eight English evil elephants
Nine nasty nutty natterjack toads
Ten terrible, ticklish tadpoles.

Julian Patient (7)
Lichfield Cathedral School

Tongue Twister

One old, orange octopus
Two terrible, tall, tame teachers
Three thankful thorny thorns
Four fast, famous flies
Five funky, fuzzy fireflies
Six sad, sweet sharks
Seven swimming, sharp swordfish
Eight electric, English, empty eels
Nine nice, neat, new newts
Ten tickled, tiny tigers.

Sam Dewsbery (7)
Lichfield Cathedral School

Anger

Anger is as red as a pen
Happiness is as happy as a rainbow
Sadness is as sad as the rain
Darkness is as dark as a hole
Lights are as bright as the sun
A monster is as green as the grass
Sol is as red as fire
Space is as black as thunder
What colour are you?

James Wyatt (7)
Lichfield Cathedral School

Happiness

What colour is it?
Happiness is as red as a rose
What does it sound like?
It sounds like happiness
What does it smell like?
It smells like chocolate
What does it taste like?
It tastes like a ripe raspberry.

Tommie Collingwood (7)
Lichfield Cathedral School

The Bogey

The monster is as green as grass
It sounds like *grrrr!*
It tastes like blood and guts
It smells like mouldy cheese
It looks like a big ball of skin
It feels like a fluffy ball
And reminds me of 'The Monster!'

Freddie Beharrell (7)
Lichfield Cathedral School

Happiness

What colour is happiness?
It's as blue as the sea
What does it sound like?
It sounds like laughing
What does it taste like?
It tastes like chocolate cake
What does it smell like?
It smells like strawberries
What does it feel like?
It feels like soft clouds
It looks like the world.

Lauren James (7)
Lichfield Cathedral School

Anger

Anger is as red as blood
Anger sounds like it's fierce
It smells like my mum's wine
It tastes like a hot chilli
It looks like red and black darkness
It reminds me of when
I was mad at my mum
It feels like goo!

William Mucklow (7)
Lichfield Cathedral School

Friendship

As white as a cloud
It sounds like the wind
It tastes like chocolate cake
It smells like roses and feels like snow
It reminds me of friends.

Annika Rabone (7)
Lichfield Cathedral School

Funny Fantasies

One orange obese octopus
Two tall toxic teachers
Three thin thorny Thunderbirds
Four fat funky frogs
Five fast famous foxes
Six savage scatty scorpions
Seven silvery sharp sharks
Eight electrical evil eels
Nine nasty nutty natterjack toads
Ten terrific terrifying tarantulas.

Dominic Sterland (7)
Lichfield Cathedral School

Silly Rhyming Songs

One old orange owl
Two terrible tiny tortoises
Three thirsty thunderbirds
Four fast famous fizzy Fantas
Five flying fancy frogs
Six see-saw songs
Seven sad sweet songs
Eight exciting elevators
Nine nice new noodles.

Oona McBride (8)
Lichfield Cathedral School

Tongue Twister

One orange, outrageous ostrich
Two talented, terrific tigers
Three thorny, thirsty Thunderbirds
Four famous, fashionable fireflies
Five fancy, fuzzy foxes
Six sharp, scary sharks
Seven small, smooth seals
Eight electric, emerald eels
Nine nice, naughty newts
Ten terrible, tender tortoises.

Lauren Ward (7)
Lichfield Cathedral School

Funny Bunny's Poem

One odd, outrageous ostrich
Two terrible, toxic, terrifying, tiny tarantulas
Three thrifty, thoughtful thunderbirds
Four funky, famous, fantastic frogs
Five flying, feathered firebirds
Six serious, sharp, scary sharks
Seven sweet, shy, secret swans
Eight exciting, emerald, English elephants
Nine naughty, neat, noble newts
Ten tender, talented, tame tortoises.

Isobel Butler (7)
Lichfield Cathedral School

Sport

There are lots of different sports to play
It's good to do some every day

On a Monday I like to go for a run
That is very good fun

On a Tuesday I go for a bike ride
And on a Wednesday dance with pride

On a Thursday I like to go for a swim
I feel like a shark without a fin

On Friday I play golf after school
And on a Saturday I'm back in the pool

On a Sunday my favourite sport of all
Is playing rugby with a funny shaped ball.

Otto Williams (8)
Lichfield Cathedral School

Happiness

What colour is it? Happiness is as red as a rose
What does it sound like? It sounds like laughter
What does it taste like? It tastes like chocolate cake
What does it smell like? It smells like a nice yummy raspberry
What does it feel like? It feels like reading a book in a warm cosy bed
Happiness is collecting shells on a sandy beach
Happiness is Father Christmas, the Easter bunny and the tooth fairy
Happiness is sharing with my friends and family
Happiness is a group hug.

Alice-Ruth Davies (7)
Lichfield Cathedral School

Tongue Twisters

One old, oblong octopus
Two terrific, tiny, tired tigers
Three thankful, thoughtful, thorny birds
Four fast, fancy, fuzzy, fun frogs
Five famous, fat, funky, furry foxes
Six sad, shy, small, smooth, sweet seals
Seven shining, sparkling sheep
Eight English, exciting eels
Nine nice, new toads
Ten tiny teddies.

Darcy Banks & Amelia Sanders (7)
Lichfield Cathedral School

Nutty Nature

One old, 'orrible orang-utans
Two terrifying, toxic teachers
Three thankful, thoughtful thunderbirds
Four fuzzy, funky foxes
Five freckled, frozen falcons
Six sad, scaly seals
Seven savage, silver scorpions
Eight elderly, exciting elephants
Nine nasty, naughty natterjack toads
Ten terrific, talented tortoises.

Dan Wakefield & William Collins (8)
Lichfield Cathedral School

Tongue Twister

One old, orange, 'orrible, oblong ostrich
Two terrible, terrific, tiny teddies
Three thankful, thin, Thunderbirds
Four fast, famous, funky, fuzzy fish
Five football flags flying
Six sad, scaly, skinny snakes
Seven scary, slimy, sharp sharks
Eight electric, English, evil, exciting elephants
Nine nasty, new, noble newts
Ten toy trombones.

Molly Hudson & Matthew Inglis (7)
Lichfield Cathedral School

My Magic Box

(Based on 'The Magic Box' by Kit Wright)

I will keep in my box . . .
A dancing snowman
The feeling of going into the Grand Canyon
And the sight of the golden sunset

I will place in my box . . .
The taste of melted chocolate
The smell of freshly baked bread
The sound of birds singing in the morning

My box is made of . . .
Gold, silver and electricity
With a lid made of chocolate
And dinosaur eyes on the top.

In my box I will . . .
Play football for England in the World Cup Final
And lay on a beach, the colour of the sun
I was a bird when I flew into my magic box.

Joe Murphy (10)
St Luke's CE Primary School, Cannock

My Magic Box
(Based on 'The Magic Box' by Kit Wright)

I will put in my box . . .
The colour of a rainbow
The taste of the sea
The tart of a lemon and
All the special things to me

The ice of a dragon
The song of a lark,
And the thrill of a ride
In an amusement park

The breast of a robin
The pumping of my heart
And the thrill of being on a
Cool go-kart.

The words of a budgie
Like the smell of a farm
Like the rumbling of thunder
That means you no harm.

My box is a safe haven for when I'm away for
All the things inside my head
That might go astray

My box is made of bronze, silver and gold
Decorated with memories and dreams,
Taking you away to dreamland.

Jacob Massey (11)
St Luke's CE Primary School, Cannock

Chloe's Magic Box

(Based on 'Magic Box' by Kit Wright)

I will place in my box . . .
The first saddle I ever used,
The first velvet dress I ever wore, my first ever chore

I will treasure in my box . . .
The first time I swam with a dolphin like a shark
My first freezing snowball fight;
When there was a golden horse insight

I will keep safe in my box . . .
When I moved up into the next group at riding,
When I first galloped on a horse
When I first learnt about force

My box will be made from beautiful golden horse skin
And the golden stirrups made of metal
I shall ride again in my box
And swim with a shark like a cunning fox.

Chloe Smith (10)
St Luke's CE Primary School, Cannock

My Magic Box

(Based on 'Magic Box' by Kit Wright)

I will carefully place in my box . . .
The beautiful golden beaches of India
My lovely black and brown dog called Sonny
And my adorable little black and white cat called Trixie
The warm locking hands of winter

I will treasure in my box . . .
My World Cup footballs that look like sparkling planets
And all my football kits, especially my new Man U kit
All my achievements, the greatest being 'Man of the Match' for
Chase Tigers

In my box I will . . .
Own a chocolate factory
Play for England and for Manchester United
And own a life of glory and fame

My box is fashioned with gold and diamond jewels
And my box is made out of memories, love and dreams.

Will Gonsalves (10)
St Luke's CE Primary School, Cannock

My Magic Box

(Based on 'Magic Box' by Kit Wright)

I shall keep in my magic box . . .
A white box full of the smells of winter
A tiny den in the Caribbean with the breeze of the sea
And the brown curls of my brother's hair

I shall keep safely in my box . . .
The taste of a juicy strawberry
Glistening in a beam of sunlight with a burst of lemon
My family whom I love to death!
And a teardrop running down my face, missing my brother

I shall treasure in my box . . .
The beautiful sea that feels like silk
A massive doughnut van saying 'Alex's' on the front
And the smell of sugar!

My box shall be made of
Pink elastic with silver rims
And gold coins as the hinges!

I shall do shows in my box
And play the electric guitar
My mum and dad will be watching me.

Alex Lloyd (10)
St Luke's CE Primary School, Cannock

My Magic Box

(Based on 'Magic Box' by Kit Wright)

I will treasure in my box . . .
The sharp blue smell of chlorine
The joy and warmth inside of me when I win a race
The touch of water droplets almost like crystals tapping me gently
And the colour of a glistening topaz blue.

I will cherish in my box . . .
A sip of joy from a magical, dazzling lake
A tear of sadness from a beautiful, tiny baby
Pitch-black velvet snow of a saturated cloud,
And the juice of an emerald lime.

My box is made of . . .
Pure, colourless water and a fragment of the night sky
Crammed with blinding stars
The hinges will be made by hands of forgiveness and love

In my box I shall . . .
Swim in the Olympics
Awake the next morning with
A glittering gold medal which I will lay gently in my box
Once again.

Christie Ghent (10)
St Luke's CE Primary School, Cannock

My Magic Box

(Based on 'Magic Box' by Kit Wright)

I will put in my box . . .
The sight of an amazing sunrise
The smell of a delicious cooked breakfast
The feeling of victory

I will put in my box . . .
The sight of an amazing New Year
The amazing, beautiful, calm, clear Spanish sea.
The flavour as a pepperoni pizza

I will put in my box . . .
An amazingly beautiful tree in Spain
The amazing sport called football
The feeling of winning
The support and company of my great friends

My box looks like . . .
A clear blue sky at night
A box with jewels on it
A crocodile when you open it

I will watch . . .
Manchester United in my box play football
I will play on my trampoline, jumping in the air
I will listen to the birds in the morning.

Sam Whitehouse (10)
St Luke's CE Primary School, Cannock

The Box Of Magic

(Based on 'Magic Box' by Kit Wright)

I will put in my box . . .
A white fluffy cloud from the sky
A tail of a dog, fluffy and cuddly
Happiness from celebrating a party

I will hide in my box . . .
The sound of a siren from a police car
A golden sun and a rainbow
A big house with a snooker table in it

I will keep store in my box . . .
A wizard on a sledge
And a boy on a flying broomstick
The sound of a bomb going off

My box is fashioned from silver and blue
With circles on the lid and secrets round the edges
Its hinges are like bendy aluminium

I shall swim in my box . . .
On the Mediterranean Sea on the
Coast of the south of France
And see all the beautiful fish.

Connor Taylor (10)
St Luke's CE Primary School, Cannock

My Magic Box

(Based on 'Magic Box' by Kit Wright)

I will place in my box . . .
The smell of a banana milkshake
The soft touch of my favourite PJs
The fingers of summer giving me a tan
And my temperature rising when Wolves win

I will lay in my box . . .
The colour of orange, my fiery temper
An owl with ears and a mouse with a beak
And an otter with a head of hair.

My box is made of . . .
Cold ice cream with stardust
It has love in the corners
Its hinges are claws of lions

I will dance in my box
Of high seas
And land on the soft back of a lion.

Katie Barnes (10)
St Luke's CE Primary School, Cannock

My Magic Box

(Based on 'Magic Box' by Kit Wright)

I will place in my box . . .
The big black eyes of my dog Ginny
The sight of my whole family
The vibrant colours of Autumn

I will place in my box . . .
The taste of lamb dinner
The noise of laughter
The feel of Ginny's fur

I will cherish in my box . . .
My favourite place
Millions of shining jewels
All my family

My box is made of black velvet with stars attached

In my box I will . . .
Fly through space in a giant spaceship
Learn how to play football brilliantly.

William Hawkins (11)
St Luke's CE Primary School, Cannock

My Magic Box

(Based on 'Magic Box' by Kit Wright)

I will place in my box . . .
The memory of some friends coming from Australia to England
The memory of having my first rabbits
And my nan's dog getting to know me really well

I will keep safely in my box . . .
The warmth of winter
A torch that shines like a star
All of my friends' pets
A snail that whizzes fast like lightning
A fish with a tail and a dog with fins
A snowman that dances and sings

My box is made of . . .
Rock and ice with stardust on the lid and shimmery diamonds
On the sides
The hinges on my box are made of the toe-joints of a polar bear

I will look after my pets and animals
In my box while I travel around the world.

Rachel Beaman (10)
St Luke's CE Primary School, Cannock

My Magic Box

(Based on 'Magic Box' by Kit Wright)

I will place in my box . . .
The bright orange cast from my leg
The first book I ever read
A troll that looks like a burnt head

I will treasure in my box . . .
The first time I saw a killer whale
When I got kissed by a sea lion
When Mum burnt herself with the iron

I will put in my box . . .
A dog with a driver's licence
A driver with a tail
And Shelly, my first ever pet snail

My box is made from killer whale skin
With all my missing baby teeth as the lid
And sounds, as the legs, from when I was a little kid

I shall swim again with dolphins in my box
Then set free a shark as cunning as a fox.

Ellen Whordley (10)
St Luke's CE Primary School, Cannock

My Magic Box

(Based on 'Magic Box' by Kit Wright)

I will treasure in my box . . .
The sparkling stars in midnight sky
Amazing wonders of the world
The hot sandy beach with the wind drifting through my toes

I will cherish in my box . . .
The first step of a baby
The last touch of an old man
A smell of popcorn just come out the microwave

My box is fashioned from
The deep crystal clear sea
The shine of diamonds placed around the sides
The lid is made by 100 pound notes

I shall swim with a dolphin in a box
And relax in a Hilton spa
With all my caring friends!

Amy McKenzie (10)
St Luke's CE Primary School, Cannock

My Magic Box

(Based on 'Magic Box' by Kit Wright)

I will put in my box . . .
The touch of Tutankhamen's golden mask
The sound of a great white shark splashing in the ocean
The smell of petrol

I will put in my box . . .
The hoot of a barn owl at night
The touch of a black panther's fur
The sound of an explosion in the distance
The taste of spaghetti carbonara

My box is fashioned from brown and red paints
With golden jewels and secrets in the corners and rubber hinges
I shall roll around in my box all over the world
And then enjoy great feasts.

Jack Plester (11)
St Luke's CE Primary School, Cannock

My Magic Box

(Based on 'Magic Box' by Kit Wright)

I will place in my box . . .
The pumpkin spooking me on Hallowe'en
The sound of fireworks going bang, bang, bang
And the happiness of a new millennium

I will treasure in my box . . .
My dog like a cheetah
My fish being a submarine
And the hope of living these things again

My box is made out of . . .
Solid gold and silver with wishes in the corner
And ice of a dragon for hinges

I shall go on holiday in my box
Whilst climbing all the mountains
And to top up my tan again with the warm gold hands of the sun.

David Cockram (10)
St Luke's CE Primary School, Cannock

My Magic Box

(Based on 'Magic Box' by Kit Wright)

I will put in my magic box . . .
The sound of the sea washing pebbles against the beach
The excitement of my first Christmas morning
The company of my best friends

I will put in my box . . .
The memory of Year 5
The excitement of moving house
The feeling of getting my first pet
The first train set I ever had
The sound, and colours of fireworks going off at night
The feeling of my tummy on the aeroplane as we take off

I will have on my box . . .
Glittery stars in the golden moonlight
I would drive in my train to the corners of the world with my box.

Shaun Gilbert (10)
St Luke's CE Primary School, Cannock

The Magic Box

(Based on 'Magic Box' by Kit Wright)

I will treasure in my box . . .
A beautiful butterfly of summer
A baby's first smell of a rose
The touch of the stickiest sweet ever

I will treasure in my box . . .
A dog drinking Coke out of a coffee cup
A gorgeous honeymoon in a Spanish villa
A game of hide-and-seek with my new cousin Eve

My box is fashioned of dust
From the peak of Mount Everest
With an 18 carat gold diamond in the middle
With corners of glittering stars

I shall sunbathe on the great
Sunny sands in my box and run
And jump into a fresh, cool, pool.

Emma Watkins (10)
St Luke's CE Primary School, Cannock

Alice's Box

(Based on 'Magic Box' by Kit Wright)

I will place in my box . . .
The slippy slime of a snail
The touch of the softest hand
A picture of a baby and its mother

I will bury in my box . . .
The sound of a Ferrari passing by,
The smell of bacon in the oven
A galloping horse winning the race

I will keep hidden in my box . . .
The first opening of the eyes of a newborn baby
The flash of lightning and a rumble of thunder
The fresh air and the bright blue sky

I will treasure in my box . . .
The great deep blue sea with life in it
The feel of dustiness from the snow
The burning of a fire-breathing dragon.

Alice Standley (10)
St Luke's CE Primary School, Cannock

Bethany's Mysterious Box

(Based on 'Magic Box' by Kit Wright)

I will place in my box . . .
The smell of smoke coming from the chimney
The sight of a warm sunset shining in my window
The texture of sandpaper

I will treasure in my box . . .
The love that my family gives to me
The excitement of Valkenberg
A plane flying over the Atlantic ocean

My box will be fashioned
With diamonds and pearls
Sweets and curls with patterns and glitter
And sparkly girls.

I shall climb with my box and hike with my box
I shall sleep with my box
I will go abroad with my box
I will make and break with my box.

That is what I will do with my box!

Bethany Evans (10)
St Luke's CE Primary School, Cannock

Kira's Magic Box

(Based on 'Magic Box' by Kit Wright)

I will treasure in my box . . .
The misty smell of winter
The last snowdrop in spring
The first leaf to fall in autumn

I will treasure in my box . . .
The first star of night
The moon shining bright
The sound of the wind

I will treasure in my box . . .
A world not hurting animals
A world beyond belief
The smell of a chocolate chip cookie

My box is made to treasure all things great and small
With moons on the lid and wishes in the corners

I shall ride my box from New York to Paris
Break world records like going all around the world
And the land of a fluffy white cloud.

Kira George (10)
St Luke's CE Primary School, Cannock

My Ocean-Blue Box

(Based on 'Magic Box' by Kit Wright)

I will cherish in my box . . .
The rich smell of orange juice in a New York morning
The first heroic man on the morning
A fluffy white snowflake from Mount Everest

I will cherish in my box . . .
A golden sacred cup, stolen by a Northern barbarian
The first bible of Britain smothered and covered in miracles
The last line in Latin written with courage

I will cherish in my box . . .
Rama the demon King with nine extra heads
The last leaf from a rich green tree
The masses of blossom from a Chinese star tree

In my box I will ride a dolphin
GO back in time with Doctor Who in the Tardis
Travel Narnia and see the White Witch and Aslan.

William Bakewell (11)
St Luke's CE Primary School, Cannock

My Mystery Box

(Based on 'Magic Box' by Kit Wright)

I will treasure in my box . . .
The first whisp of snow in winter
The smells of World War II with a hint of mist
The feel of Niagara Falls with a spray of cold, misty water

I will treasure in my box . . .
Hints of the colours of the rainbow
Seashells rubbing against the salty sea
I will hide in my box the shadows of the world

I will treasure in my box . . .
The glide of a glittering, shimmering wave colliding against the rocks
The heat of a flame-thrower being switched on and off
The sight of a shooting star from the corner of my eye

I will treasure in my box . . .
The swish of a knitted jumper with sashes of lace
The cold ice rink with glittering shimmering colours above
The sound of the rain falling on the leaves.

Chanelle Tranter (11)
St Luke's CE Primary School, Cannock

In My Magic Box I Will Put

(Based on 'Magic Box' by Kit Wright)

In my magic box I will put . . .
A rescued dinosaur saved from extinction
A magic wand enchanted with a spell
An afternoon of fun relived in every way

I will treasure in my box . . .
A medicine from the future to save lives
A volcanic eruption never to happen again
A medieval bow still warm from battle

I will put in and never take out of my box . . .
A knight's armour with the aroma of death
A key to everything opening every door
A universe beyond imagination

In my box I will go anywhere doing anything
It's crafted with wood and timber, the greatest secret is itself
In my box is a journey of a lifetime.

Connor Bates (10)
St Luke's CE Primary School, Cannock

My Magical Box

(Based on 'Magic Box' by Kit Wright)

I will bury in my box . . .
Tentacles from an octopus from the dark sea
Secrets hidden in each and every corner
The reflection of a moon into a shiny lake

I will hide in my box . . .
A sunset from a beautiful summer's night
The life of the donkey that Mary rode on
And the sound of waves swishing onto the shore

I will keep in my box . . .
The sight of sweet-shaped stars
The smell of melted chocolate
And the sight of a gold engagement ring

I will play ball games in my box
Outside on green grass just put down
And I will play on the beach like I did in my childhood.

Megan Shirley (10)
St Luke's CE Primary School, Cannock

My Box

(Based on 'Magic Box' by Kit Wright)

I will put in my box . . .
A feather of a snowy white dove
A rainbow of many pretty colours
The sparkle of a million stars from above

I will put in my box . . .
The scent of newly grown flowers
The smell of new air and old air
The colourful smoke coming out of the black and white chimney

I will put in my box . . .
My family so when I am sad I can talk to them
The smell of my dad's work helmet which reminds me of him

My box is made of wood, steel and plastic
With pictures of my family on it
The hinges are made of rabbit claws

I will play in my box and I will treasure it until I die.

Amber Parkes (10)
St Luke's CE Primary School, Cannock

Jessica's Magic Box

(Based on 'Magic Box' by Kit Wright)

I will treasure in my box . . .
The first snowflake of winter
The last leaf of winter
And the swishing sound of the sparkling river

I will keep in my box . . .
A twinkling star from the night sky
A snowy white cloud from the light blue sky
And the heat from the boiling hot sun

I will hide in my box . . .
The first living creature of the Earth
The smell of chocolate chip cookies coming out of the oven
The feel of a black and white stripy zebra

I will take my box . . .
To the deep dark sea with all the fish
Then fly into the sky as fast as an eagle
And land on a fluffy white cloud.

Jessica Hodgkiss (10)
St Luke's CE Primary School, Cannock

Kieran's Magical Box

(Based on 'Magic Box' by Kit Wright)

I will place in my box . . .
The sensitive icy touch of a misty hidden lake
An orange glowing piece of the sun
The black hole of two partial worlds colliding

I will store in my box . . .
The werewolf howl on a full moon
The first quiet step on the moon
The colourful loud atmosphere of the World Cup final

I will fashion my box . . .
By the first glowing star that had been wished on
The scales of a fish to spell my initials
The cold rock from the top of Mount Everest to store it in

I shall drive in my box . . .
All day in Ferrari Enzo along the Swiss Alps
Going at the amazing speed of 210 mph.

Kieran Evans (11)
St Luke's CE Primary School, Cannock

The Magic Box

(Based on 'Magic Box' by Kit Wright)

I will put in the box . . .
My first glance of a rainbow
The taste of a hot chocolate drink
And the feeling of a wobbly tooth

I will put in the box . . .
The sound of birds singing in spring
The smell of a McDonald's on my plate
The thought of winning the lottery.

The hinges are made of dragons' teeth . . .
The lid is made of gold
And the corners made of steel
I will go power shooting in my box
And swim when it is dark.

Bradley Davies (10)
St Luke's CE Primary School, Cannock

The Magic Box

(Based on 'Magic Box' by Kit Wright)

I will treasure in my box . . .
The smell of the salty sea
The feel of a snowflake drifting from the sky
Three crystal wishes spoken in Dutch

I will bury in my box . . .
A rainbow created from fairy dust
A sip from the wide open Atlantic
A snowman made on the top of Mount Everest

I will cherish in my box . . .
A teacher to teach me all about Ancient history
A feather from a great white dove
A magical rose petal, the colour pink

I will surf on my box and land on golden sand
I will take my box and have great adventures in Spain.

Katie O'Mahoney (10)
St Luke's CE Primary School, Cannock

Phil's Mad Box

(Based on 'Magic Box' by Kit Wright)

I will store in my box . . .
The smell of petrol from a new petrol station
The smell of a brand new car
Then the smell of a newly caught sea bass

I will bury in my box . . .
The feel of a boat hitting a great big wave
The feel of holding a newborn baby.

I will treasure in my box . . .
The first words of my mum and dad
Three wishes from a magic genie
The last smile of Mr Blobby.

My box is made out of platinum and lead
The bottom is made out of sweets and home-made sponge cake.

Philip Bell (10)
St Luke's CE Primary School, Cannock

My Magic Box

(Based on 'Magic Box' by Kit Wright)

I will put in my box . . .
The smell of a brand new day
My first taste of an ice cream
The sound of my baby brother laughing

I will put in my box . . .
The sound of my mum pouring ice-cold water in my glass
The touch of the cold sea on my toes
The sweet taste of apple pie and custard

I will put in my box . . .
The sight of a snowman melting
The sound of my mum speaking to me
The touch of a newborn sheep

My box is fashioned with pink cover on top
With jewels all around with diamonds.

Abi Cartwright (10)
St Luke's CE Primary School, Cannock

My Magic Box

(Based on 'Magic Box' by Kit Wright)

I will cherish in my box . . .
The taste of chocolate in the morning
The smell of creamy hot chocolate late at night
The feeling of scoring the winning goal in a World Cup final

I shall lay in my box . . .
Everlasting friendship
The sight of a gorilla scratching its head
A sunny day when the sun is so clear
It is a yellow beach ball in the sky

My box is carved out of pure chocolate
It has legs of gold and handles of hard sweets

I shall play football with gorillas in my box
I shall play hockey with a chocolate bar
I shall skydive from a sky so blue it could have been painted.

Daniel Hyde (10)
St Luke's CE Primary School, Cannock

My Magical Box

(Based on 'Magic Box' by Kit Wright)

I will put in my box . . .
The sunset on a sandy desert
The sight of a fluffy cloud resembling a snowman
The life of a great white shark beneath the deep blue sea

I will hide in my box . . .
A twinkling star from the heavens above
My younger days when I built castles in the sand
The moon shining lovingly down at me

I will bury in my box . . .
The sound of birds tweeting on a Sunday morning
The scent of Mum's perfume
The shine of a wedding ring.

I will live in my box . . .
Like a genie does and people rub my box so I can pop out
I will look after my box until the day I die.

Rowen Wort (10)
St Luke's CE Primary School, Cannock

My Magic Box

(Based on 'Magic Box' by Kit Wright)

I will put in my magic box . . .
The winning goal of my football team
The smell of fish and chips on a Friday night
My first day at primary school.

I will put in my box . . .
My mom's smile when I'm very good
The flame of fire from my fire light
A bullet's whizz as it's fired from a gun.

I will put in my box . . .
The smell of a freshly cut apple
A magic car that can dance and
The thought of going on holiday.

My box is made of metal flames and has
Red diamonds all over it.
I will make my box my own room
And watch TV all day.

Christopher Keeley (10)
St Luke's CE Primary School, Cannock

My Magic Box

(Based on 'Magic Box' by Kit Wright)

I will place in my box . . .
The sound of a thousand horses galloping on water,
The last wish of a grandma
A book containing all my secrets

I will treasure in my box . . .
All of my friend's pets
A torch made from a star
A turtle that is as fast as lightning
And a fifth and sixth season

I will keep safely in my box . . .
A baby's first laugh
A porcupine with fur and a dog with spikes
And a snowman that talks

My box is made of ice, with stardust on the lid and
Sunbeams in the corners
Its hinges will be the beaks of wild dodos.

I will go skiing in my box from the peaks of the French Alps
And swim in the Atlantic Ocean, then wash up on
a sunny beach in Spain

Dionne Drysdale (10)
St Luke's CE Primary School, Cannock

My Magic Box

(Based on 'Magic Box' by Kit Wright)

I will keep safe in my box . . .
The memory of my dead sister
The glorious taste of ketchup
And a flying pig

I will treasure in my box . . .
The sight of Wales
The look of John Cena and Hulk Hogan
And the smell of chocolate cake

I will cherish safe in my box . . .
I will cherish my mobile as it was my own flesh and blood
My house that is comfy to live in
And also my best friend, Liam

My box is made of the finest scarlet-red bubblegum
It has chocolate on the top of the lid
And hinges made of sweets

I shall play snooker in my box
While the rippling waves of the crystal bath
Water splash over me.

Zach Harrison (10)
St Luke's CE Primary School, Cannock

My Magic Box

(Based on 'Magic Box' by Kit Wright)

I will put in my box . . .
The humour of my father
And the music of my mother
The smile of my sister
And the singing of my brother

I will place in my box . . .
The tinkering and speed
Of my rabbit I call Smudge
The cuteness and the softness
Of my guinea pig called Fudge

I will put in my box . . .
The memories of a summer's day that never ends
The taste of a massive ice cream
And the fellowship of friends

My box itself is made of gold
Found by dwarves in the darkest mine
The lid is made of sunbeams
The only box of its kind

I'd play football in my box at Molineux
And score the winning goal
I'll take England to Euro 2008
And we'll be in control.

Nick Allen (10)
St Luke's CE Primary School, Cannock

My Magic Box

(Based on 'Magic Box' by Kit Wright)

I will place in my box . . .
The cheering crowds as Manchester City win the cup
The excitement of Clare's new baby being born.
The sight of my nan getting the Fifa 2007 PlayStation game.

I will put in my box . . .
The smell of Indian food wafting across my nostrils
The pleasing voice of Mrs Griffiths saying 'Well done
Elliott, 20 out of 20 for your spelling test.'
My friend's pleased face as they achieved Level 4 SATs results . . .

I will put in my box . . .
The taste of pizza straight from Italy
The thought of a hot and sunny England
People suffering from cancer and disease and being cured

My box is fashioned from
A Manchester City sticker on the front of my lid
A picture of Clare's baby when it comes
A photo of my big sister in her black jumper
When she is in Year 10.

In my box I will be a . . .
Goalkeeper for Manchester City and not let any goals in
And I will stay friends with all my friends when I leave school
I will always be good, polite, and I will
Never lie or let anyone down.

Elliott Thurstance (10)
St Luke's CE Primary School, Cannock

My Magic Box

(Based on 'Magic Box' by Kit Wright)

I will put in my box . . .
A hundred dancing pixies sparking like fireworks in the night sky
The feeling of a loving cuddle
The excitement of my first swim

I will put in my box . . .
The scrumptious taste of a rich creamy chocolate chip ice cream
The feeling of my first tooth appearing
The glory of seeing England lift the World Cup

I will put in my box . . .
The warmth of my cosy bed on a cold winter's night
The touch of a frozen caveman sitting on a rock
The taste of a freshly made banana split

My box is decorated in dragons' claws
Monster teeth and it is surrounded by fire
It smells like warm hot chocolate
It looks like a magical masterpiece of art

In my box I will climb Mount Everest with my whole family
and all my friends.

Adam Cardno (10)
St Luke's CE Primary School, Cannock

My Magic Box

(Based on 'Magic Box' by Kit Wright)

I will put in my box . . .
The sounds my cat makes as he watches the birds
The taste of my first cup of tea
The sound of my friends on the playground

I will put in my box . . .
The smell of a home cooked dinner
The crashing of the sea against the rocks
The ice-cold shudder of a cold drink

I will put in my box . . .
The sound of exciting music
The aroma of freshly baked bread
The taste of freshly cooked fish and chips

My box is fashioned with seashells and rubies and diamonds
The lid with shark teeth on.

I will swim in my box in the big sea
I throw a party in my box
The biggest party can be
I shall love my box!

Jade McLaughlin (10)
St Luke's CE Primary School, Cannock

My Magic Box

(Based on 'Magic Box' by Kit Wright)

I will put in my box . . .
The sound of children playing in the park
The sight of Liverpool winning the Premiership
The excitement of being born

I will put in my box . . .
The taste of my first dinner my mum cooked for me
The sound of laughing,
The sound of the birds waking me first thing in the morning

I will put in my box . . .
The tingling feeling of me going on the first roller coaster
The sound of my friends talking to me
The sound of people cheering children at sports day

My box looks like . . .
The summer breeze of spring
It looks like all of the countries put together
My box is made of all the love in my heart

In my box . . .
I will play for my country and my team
I will go to London and see the fireworks on New Year's Eve
And have a good time at Alton Towers.

Ryan McCulloch (10)
St Luke's CE Primary School, Cannock

The Magic Box

(Based on 'Magic Box' by Kit Wright)

I will put in my box . . .
The first kiss off my mum when she wakes me up
The excitement I feel on Christmas morning
The scrumptious taste of sausage wrapped in bacon

I will put in my box . . .
The steam of the kettle early in the morning
The smell of fish and chips for tea
The taste of candyfloss in my mouth

I will put in my box . . .
The noise from the crowd when England scores
A Ford Mustang GT engine revving up
The smell of Connor's shoes in the morning

My box is made of soft bird feathers
The lock is made of glass
In the corners are spiders' webs

I am going to play cards in my box with my best friend Elliott
And destroy the darkness altogether.

Sam Figurski (10)
St Luke's CE Primary School, Cannock

My Magic Box

(Based on 'The Magic Box' by Kit Wright)

I will put in my box . . .
The first smile of my baby cousin.
Flashing his two new teeth as they sparkle
The taste of my first chocolate bar
My memories of my first baby toy.

I will put in my box . . .
The smell of freshly cooked fish and chips
A snowy night with a glistening moon
A first cup of tea of the day.

I will put in my box . . .
The feeling of the first Hallowe'en
A glistening lake at night
The loud bark of a dog
The first sight of deer at Cannock Chase.

My box is made out of pirate's gold
With gems on the top and for the hinges . . .
A calm lake.

I shall ride a horse on the beach
Galloping towards the horizon
And be graceful, like a swan
With my box.

Megan Thompson (10)
St Luke's CE Primary School, Cannock

My Magic Box

(Based on 'Magic Box' by Kit Wright)

I will put in my box . . .
The memory of Aston Villa winning the Carling Cup
The smell of a cooked dinner as I walk in from school
The delicious flavour of shiny oysters

I will put in my box . . .
The smooth blue sky of Torquay
The enthusiastic school choir
Getting my first 'Man of the Match' for Chase Tigers

I will put in my box . . .
The thrill of my first birthday
The feeling of standing amongst an 80,000 Wembley crowd
The delicious taste of any pizza

In my box I will be at the Millennium Stadium
Seeing Villa play
Me tasting the biggest pizza ever
Remembering my first birthday
Going on my first holiday abroad.

Jack Wright (11)
St Luke's CE Primary School, Cannock

My Magic Box

(Based on 'The Magic Box' by Kit Wright)

I will treasure in my box . . .
When I ran out on to the Molineux pitch
That is a smooth carpet of green,
Walking in and seeing the enormous Millennium Stadium,
Feeling the buzz when Wolves won the play-offs
In Cardiff.

I will place carefully in my box . . .
The sound of the roaring stock car engines
With rumbling bellies at Rockingham,
The thrill of learning to ride my bike,
The excitement of learning to swim.

I will keep safely in my box . . .
The first sight of my rabbit and his golden fur glistening like a star,
Seeing the glorious Oxford buildings where my sister is living,
Enjoying my first day at school and making loads of new friends.

I will fashion my box with . . .
Snow and ice,
With cobwebs in the corners,
And shark teeth for hinges.

In my box I will . . .
Score the winning goal in the World Cup Final,
Sink the winning putt at the Ryder Cup,
And take the winning catch in the Ashes!

Richard Jones (11)
St Luke's CE Primary School, Cannock

My Magic Box

(Based on 'The Magic Box' by Kit Wright)

I will place in my box . . .
A taste of Spain with its boiling hot sun,
The cool swimming pool when I dive in
And a big wave from the Mediterranean Sea

I will treasure in my box . . .
All of the memories of my friends
In England, when I move to Spain
The arguments and rows with my sister,
But always making up again.

I will cherish in my box . . .
Pictures of my aunties, uncles and friends,
My diary with my secrets and secret things inside,
And my first ever book, 'The Goldfish.'

My box is made of . . .
Wood, with lots of sequins and materials like velvet and felt.
Inside of my box it will be made of pictures I have drawn,
Like flowers.

In my box I will . . .
Sunbathe on a sandy golden beach
I will build a snowman with a carrot nose,
Twig arms, and a cold nose.

Siobhan Bradbury (10)
St Luke's CE Primary School, Cannock

My Magic Box

(Based on 'The Magic Box' by Kit Wright)

I will put in my box . . .
The scent of fresh smelling flowers
My rabbit called Mopsy
And my bird called Basil

I will place in my box . . .
All of my favourite toys
And all my games including
My computer.

I will put in my box . . .
All of my photos around my bedroom,
The TV,
And my family

I will stack in my box . . .
All of my work that I have done
In the past few years.

Samuel Diesbergen (10)
St Luke's CE Primary School, Cannock

Darth Vader

A red light
Darth Vader's sword
Buttons all over his tummy
The force in his hands.

Dressed in black
His helmet shines
He battles Kenobi
And wins.

Ross Perry (7)
St Peters Primary School, Yoxall

The World

I was in space
It was a weird place
I fell asleep
And heard something leap
Woke up with a fright
It was the middle of the night
Then flew my way home
The first thing I saw was a rusty old gnome
And the spring flowers
But rusty old towers
At night I saw the stars in the sky
And saw a bird flying high
Then saw a dog
And it was in the fog
I walked by the river
And did a little shiver
I saw a fox
Lying in a box
I saw a boy kicking a ball.

Katie Burbridge (7)
St Peters Primary School, Yoxall

My Mum

My mum she's like a flower whose petals do not come off
She brings light to our life
She brings that laughter sound to our voice
Somewhere in my heart I know she is right
She brings the fair to life, the rides spinning round,
The lights shining so bright.
My mum is the best.

Emily Cleary (8)
St Peters Primary School, Yoxall

Waiting For My Tea!

The horses were grunting like a pig
The dogs were barking like a wolf
The dolphins were squeaking like a mouse
The cats were climbing on the window sill.

The clouds were growing dark
The sky was bright
The breeze was as cold as ice
My mum was making rice and it sounded nice.

My brother was playing with his fire engine
My mum was making the tea
My dad was on his phone and nearly tripped over me.

My next-door neighbour asked to play with me
My brother wanted to go on his bike
But mum said, 'No, because it's time for tea.'

Ellen Rutherford (8)
St Peters Primary School, Yoxall

All About Bobby

Bobby is fluffy and scruffy
Bobby is lovely and cuddly
He likes to play hide-and-seek when we go
On a walk every week
He has black eyes that match the night skies
Bobby has sharp teeth, he likes to eat beef
Bobby has a rock solid head and he likes to go in his bed,
He only barks, he can't talk
But he can always tell us when he wants a walk,
He likes to play with us every day.

James Bell (7)
St Peters Primary School, Yoxall

Hallowe'en

Pumpkins glowing with scary faces
People running away scared
Mouths zig-zagged, triangle noses
And eyes that watch and stare.

Witches zooming across the misty sky
On wooden whizzing brooms
Skeletons rising from the grave
Rattling around their tombs.

Spiders creeping around the windows
Wrapping up their tea
Bats screeching and flapping their wings
Heading back to their spooky tree.

Harvey Marples (7)
St Peters Primary School, Yoxall

My Mate Raff

My mate is as big as house, as brown as a bear
Although he is fluffy, his tail is stronger than my dad
His growl is like thunder, his nose wet as a river,
And his feet as big as plates.

His face is always smiling, with never a frown
His eyes bright and sparkly, he is my best friend
He looks at me kindly, his head on my knee
He takes me for walks, across fields and through woods
He is always there beside me
My mate Rafferty!

Lydia Hart (8)
St Peters Primary School, Yoxall

Jack Frost

It was a cold, cold night in the middle of October
And Jack was about to bite
The trees were rocking to and fro
The owls were howling and the foxes were about
I lay shivering in my bed listening
To the noises from the middle of the night
And I knew that Jack was about to bite.
I woke in the morning to feel the bite
My toes were frozen like a block of ice
My nose was runny, my eyes were sticky,
That's what you get from a cold, cold night.

Robert Carr (8)
St Peters Primary School, Yoxall

Princess

P arties for princesses are ballroom dances, music bands and a
   creamy chocolate cake.
R ich princesses have all the money in the world
I mpolite princesses are rude to each other by hitting each other.
N eat pretty dresses are hanging in the clean dressing room.
C ats in the palace have black, smooth, glossy fur.
E xciting news from their butler they are getting 5 new
   swimming pools
S pecial dresses for an up-and-coming wedding
S ister of the bride, how much fun it's going to be!

Hanna Fletcher (7)
St Peters Primary School, Yoxall

A Peaceful Night

The stars were twinkling
They shine like the morning sun
Dolphins sleep peacefully
Fish swim around
Waves hit the shore
The moon shines
The trees sway in the wind
Cars rest on the drive
Candles burn
Crystals glow
Fingers typing
People talking.

Lauren Wood (8)
St Peters Primary School, Yoxall

Swimming

When you go swimming
Your arm reaches high
Almost as high as the sky

If you're swimming in the pool
You might meet lots of
Children from your school

I jump off the side and into the pool
Going deep in the water just like a fool.

When it's time to go
I always do my swimming slow.

Francesca Browne (8)
St Peters Primary School, Yoxall

Dreaming

Every night when I go to bed
Lots of wishes whiz round my head
I love to dream about fairies so tiny
With silky dresses and wings that are shiny
Then it is princesses in tall pink towers
Waiting for their handsome prince for hours and hours
Soon Cinderella loses her glass slippers
But will Prince Charming still like her in swimming flippers?

Next I like the story of Snow White
But sometimes that nasty queen gives me a terrifying fright
When Sleeping Beauty fell asleep
No one thought she was counting sheep
Beauty and the Beast is one of the best
But don't forget Shrek and all the rest.

Eleana O'Hare (9)
The Mosley Primary School

African Safari

Rhinos charge,
Elephants barge,
Birds flutter,
Chimpanzees mutter.

Leopards whine,
Giraffes walk in line,
Lions roar,
And those greedy warthogs just want more.

Hyenas laugh,
Hippos bath,
Snakes slide,
And crocodiles glide.

Callum Gibson (9)
The Mosley Primary School

Fairyland

A wicked witch cast a spell,
Something made an awful smell!
In Fairyland all's not well.

Cinderella's eating a chocolate dipper,
Hansel's lost his crystal slipper,
Sleeping Beauty's hair turned ginger,
Snow White's pricked her finger.

Fairy Godmother waved her wand
Cinderella finds her slipper,
Hansel's ate his chocolate dipper
Sleeping Beauty's pricked her finger
Snow White's hair turned ginger.

And suddenly they all awoke
To find it was an awful joke.

Natasha Ebbutt (9)
The Mosley Primary School

Fairy Tales

Ever since I was very small,
Fairy tales I liked them all,
Starts with people happy or sad,
Chance encounters good or bad,
Stories of witches, treasures and greed
Golden eggs and magic seeds!

Witches and wizards and giant cats,
Umbrellas and big fancy hats,
Queens and kings and small hairy things,
Dragons with fire and beating wings,
Happy ending, never sad
Good always wins, never bad.

Caitlin Wright (9)
The Mosley Primary School

Fred The Dragon

I have a dragon as a pet
He was very hard to get
He was stuck in a cave
To rescue him I had to be brave.

I was worried that I might die
I didn't want to frizzle or fry
I shouldn't have worried
I shouldn't have been scared
But sometimes I wonder why I have dared.

He's clumsy and dopey,
Smelly and big.
When he was small he liked to dig
He wrecked the garden
He wrecked the plants
He wrecked the shed and ate my pants.

At other times
He's my best mate
Everyone thinks he is great
He flies with grace
He flies with pace
He flies me all over the place.

Matthew Holmes (10)
The Mosley Primary School

Puppy Love

My dog Pippin is very clever
He is the very best dog ever
I think he's great and rather cool
Splashing and jumping in the pool.

Going on a walk is lots of fun,
Especially when there's lots of sun
He brings a stick home just for keeps
Stored in the garage, there are heaps

He wakes me up with a great big lick
Charging around like a lunatic
Pippin sits down and gives a paw
Ask again and he gives more

When he's good he gets a treat
His face is oh, so very sweet
He has a shiny little nose
Which snuffles and snores when he has a doze.

I love him and he loves me,
Come to my house and you will see
Knock on the door and step inside,
If he's frightened he will hide.

Lewis Brittain (9)
The Mosley Primary School

My Rainy Day

I look through my window at the rain coming down
And I feel myself beginning to frown
Can't go out and have fun to play
It seems that it just rains every day
Let me see what else I can do
How about something with cardboard, paint and glue?
I can make a dazzling castle fit for a mighty king
In the courtyard a pretty maiden would sing
There would be a fine prince, handsome and strong
And I a beautiful princess with hair gold and long
A fierce dragon would catch me and lock me in a dark tower
It would roar and breathe fire making me cower
But the prince would rescue me on his trusted steed
And killing the dragon would be his good deed
Off we would ride back to the castle
For fizzy pop after all that hassle
Suddenly my daydream has broke
My mum's just come in and given me a poke
'Look outside, the rain has begun to stop,
So put on your coat and off to the shop!'

Kyla Hyslop (10)
The Mosley Primary School

My Pet Unicorn

As the land is hushed with a magical aura
And the day has turned to dusk
The moon is smiling in the garden pond
With reflections glowing from way beyond.

Dancing, prancing in the sky
He's so beautiful I can't lie
His wings they shine just like new
Will he make my dreams come true?
Let the magic of this spell
Ring out like a twinkling bell.

The moonbeam shines on his horn and hooves
As he flies across the silvery roofs
So silently he moves in flight
Like a painted butterfly or kite
He whinnies blowing a velvety kiss
His gossamer wings I really miss.

Annabelle Eaton (10)
The Mosley Primary School

Animal Capers

Monkeys like to swing around
And barely ever touch the ground
They make a loud and howling noise
And play with sticks as though they're toys

Elephants are so large and grey
All must move out of the way
They splash about in swampy pools
To keep themselves nice and cool

Tigers like to creep and prowl
And also have a mighty growl
Baby tigers like to play
Having fun throughout the day.

Hippos sink down in the mud
It makes them feel very good
They could stay in there all day
Wallowing the hours away.

Giraffes are very tall and thin
Although they don't go to the gym
They reach up high into the trees
To munch and crunch acacia leaves.

Adam Parsons (9)
The Mosley Primary School

Rapunzel's Tower

Have you ever wondered why
Rapunzel's in a tower
Maybe it's because she's no
Springtime flower.

She's got dirt in her hair
And her clothes are scruffy
She's got cobwebs on and
Her room is stuffy.

In the corner of her room is her
Own loud speaker.
Sending pulses through the old
Floorboards that are growing weaker and weaker.

All her bedclothes and curtains are
Thick with grime
She says she would wash them
But she doesn't have time.

When it comes to rescuers there
Are none to be found
Because they've all fled
From miles around.

Maybe Rapunzel will grow out of this phase
Though maybe she'll stay in the
Tower for the rest of her days.

Rachel Frame (11)
The Mosley Primary School

Fairy Tales

I'm going to write a poem, now let me think . . . !
What about fairies, unicorns and pirates that sink,
Talking about pixies and magic rings,
How about wicked queens and handsome kings.

Precious golden tickets and Oompah Loompas in the sky,
Mouth-watering chocolate rivers and elevators that fly.

Augustus Gloop (who eats like a pig)
Veruca Salt (who wears a silly wig)
Violet Beauregarde (whose jaws are fit)
Mike Teevee (who wears guns for a kit).

Now you want to be a poet,
I just know it!

Eleanor Bradley (9)
The Mosley Primary School

Jack!

I have a cat called Jack, what is so special about that?
For a start he's black and he's my cat
He lies on his back, my, he's so lazy
And when he's hungry he miaows like crazy!
So I feed him a great cat feast
And he eats like a beast
Afterwards he sleeps like a baby
Dreaming about catching mice . . .maybe?
Whilst in reality he goes out and hunts for a snack
Watch out rabbits, mice and birds, he's about to attack!
Squeak, squeak, as he brings in a mouse
'*Jack get that out of the house!*'

Ben Barrett (10)
The Mosley Primary School